LINCOLN
CENTER FOR THE
PERFORMING ARTS

by Ralph G. Martin

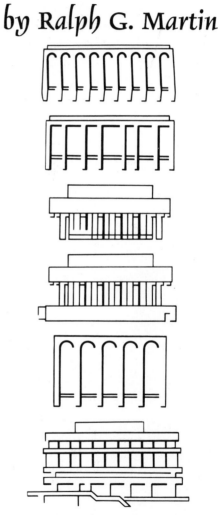

PRENTICE-HALL, INC.

ENGLEWOOD CLIFFS, NEW JERSEY

For Pearl and Allen Pastel:
Lincoln Center enriched their lives just as
they have enriched mine

This book is also dedicated to Carin,
that lonely voice
who loved music and theater;
and to Esme and Arthur, who loved Carin

LINCOLN CENTER FOR THE PERFORMING ARTS
by Ralph G. Martin

Copyright © 1971 by Ralph G. Martin

ISBN 0-13-536748-4 (casebound)

ISBN 0-13-536730-1 (paperback)

Library of Congress Catalog Card Number: 78-126827

Printed in the United States of America T

Prentice-Hall International, Inc., London
Prentice-Hall of Australia, Pty. Ltd., Sydney
Prentice-Hall of Canada, Ltd., Toronto
Prentice-Hall of India Private Ltd., New Delhi
Prentice-Hall of Japan, Inc., Tokyo

Acknowledgment is made for permission to reprint
an excerpt from *Balanchine*, by Bernard Taper
(Harper & Row, New York, 1963).

ACKNOWLEDGMENTS

First and foremost, my thanks to my friend Tom Mathews, who urged me to write this book and who should have written it with me.

My deep appreciation also to Jack de Simone and John O'Keefe, whose constant cooperation helped make this book possible.

Susanne Faulkner deserves special thanks for helping me assemble the photographs and acting as a liaison with many of the photographers.

Shirley and Paul Green were helpful, as always, in many ways.

My gratitude also to a long list of people for a variety of assistance: Jack Frizzele, Bernice Price, Doreen Lown, Si Bourgin, Susan Schulman, Bernard Taper, Elizabeth Firth, Rose Bozin, David Bennett, Cecilia Maguire, Susan Bloch, Frank Milburn, Francis Robinson, Virginia Donaldson, Mark Senigo, Helen Sullivan, Mary Keppel, Goldie and Jerry Moonelis, Josephine Graziano, among many others.

And my thanks, once again, to Mari Walker who has the taxing job of transcribing all my tape-recorded interviews and typing my manuscript. My thanks also to Dick Walker for all his help and kindness.

Mrs. Christine Lane of the Oyster Bay Public Library was again most helpful in providing necessary research material, and I add my gratitude to Richard N. Powdrell, Director of the Oyster Bay Library, and some of his staff: Annette S. Macedonio, Dee Atkinson, Gene McGrath, Ellen Coschignano, Gloria Hanrahan and Laura Lucchesi.

A personal note of appreciation to my editor, Cecile Grossman, and to my wife, Marjorie, both of whom are superb critics.

CONTENTS

introduction

If your first view of Lincoln Center were on a soft summer night, the mood would seem almost magical—the spectacular fountain with its play of lights, the dimly lit outdoor cafes, the tinkle of champagne glasses and laughter from the balconies above, the shifting mural of people beyond the glass walls.

In all this, the fountain provides the focus. And to view the scene in the plaza around it is to watch a kaleidoscope of pleasure: an elderly lady staring enthralled at the changing patterns of the fountain as if they reflected her own special visions; an aristocratic gentleman with homburg and umbrella who paces impatiently back and forth, momentarily diverted each time he passes the fountain; a heavy-set man with a broad face and open shirt, his elaborate camera on a tripod facing the fountain, clicking the shutter again and again and again.

It is nearly curtain time and now the area around the fountain is crowded with clusters of people, the quiet transformed into a hum of conversation, and then a buzzing as the people group, regroup, rush off to the different theaters. A young man sits impatiently on the rim of the fountain. Suddenly a lovely girl races into the area, her long hair swinging, her face aglow. The young man grabs her, lifts her high, kisses her again and again as she laughs and laughs, and then both run excitedly toward a theater, their laughter lingering in the plaza.

Soon the scene is quiet again, the plaza nearly deserted. But if you wait long enough, the silence suddenly explodes. The concert is over, the play, the ballet, the opera are ended: All the doors open and the people stream out, exhilarated, moving quickly and talking loudly, the sounds merging into a hectic cacophony. And through it all can be heard the joyous squeals of two little girls delighting in the spray of the fountain on their faces.

Then, just as suddenly, they are all gone—the cafe tables empty, the plaza deserted, and all that remains is the sense of place and the mood of magic.

How did it all begin?

The idea was unique. No country in the world had ever produced such a cultural center—not simply a grouping of buildings, its overall concept was bigger than any of its parts. In the early 1950's the plan was without parallel—now almost a hundred cities have taken Lincoln Center as a model for their own cultural centers.

More than a century ago, Alexis de Tocqueville observed that Americans are the most peculiar people in the world. He noted that if a citizen in a local community feels that some need is not being met, he goes across the street and discusses it with his neighbor. Soon a committee forms to function on behalf of that need. But what is most remarkable, said de Tocqueville, is that all this is done without reference to any bureaucrat—it is done by private citizens on their own initiative.

In essence, that is the foundation of the Lincoln Center dream.

It was really an old dream. In the 1930's Charles Spofford, a young member of the Metropolitan Opera Board of Directors, discussed the need for a new opera house with the fiery, music-loving Mayor of New York City, Fiorello H. LaGuardia. "What we really need," the Mayor said, "is a music center, a place where music of all kinds will be performed, and maybe the New York Philharmonic will join in—something like that!"

It was an off-the-cuff idea, but Charles Spofford was excited by it. A bright young lawyer from St. Louis, a graduate of Yale and Harvard, Spofford was to become a brigadier general in World War II, a prime mover in the Council on Foreign Relations, a director on the Board of The Juilliard School of Music, United States ambassador on a dozen important international missions. Spurred on by Mayor LaGuardia's concept, Spofford approached the Chairman of the Board of the New York Philharmonic, who told him, "There's nothing to it. Don't waste your time. It would cost more money than any of us can afford."

Parks Commissioner Robert Moses then vehemently opposed the idea. In a heated report to LaGuardia, Moses wrote that opera was a dying art form supported by a "bunch of social climbers," and the mayor "shouldn't touch it with a barge pole." The report was filed, the idea officially forgotten.

But Charles Spofford did not forget. Spofford is one of the small group of anonymous "Dukes of New York," who serve on most of the boards of most of the city's major public institutions. These Dukes are some of the busiest, most important men in New York, men who know how to move with each other, and, more importantly, how to make others move. They are men who make time for what they believe in and know how to make that time mean something. What they do is not for the sake of public recognition, but for the challenge, the sense of inner satisfaction, the commitment to public service.

An anonymous poet wrote:

A nation without great Dukes starves and dies,
And leaves a silent desert neath the skies.

Ten years passed and William O'Dwyer was now Mayor of New York. Spofford suggested to the Mayor—who was also a music lover—how nice it would be if the city were to help build a new Metropolitan Opera House in a corner of Central Park. O'Dwyer liked the idea, but advised Spofford, "First you'll have to take it up with Bob Moses." The Mayor called Moses to set up an appointment, and Moses was curt: "If he wants to put it in Central Park, tell him to save his carfare."

Spofford went to see Moses anyway. He reminded the Commissoner of the report in which he had called opera a dying art, and yet here it was ten years later, flourishing and stronger than ever.

Robert Moses is a big man with a big mind, more of a political Prince than a Duke, and never anonymous. To a large portion of the New York public, he is a driving extrovert with a sharp bite and an "edifice complex." More than any one man in New York, Moses has made his mark—a physical impact of incredible scope: bridges, tunnels, roads, parks and parkways, power projects and everything from Jones Beach and the Coliseum to the World's Fair. A graduate of Yale and Oxford with a degree in philosophy, Robert Moses has a reputation for short temper, rough language and broad imagination.

Spofford's fresh approach for a new Metropolitan Opera House captivated Moses and stirred his imagination. Congress had recently passed a Federal Housing Act for Slum Clearance. Title I of the Act allowed a city to condemn slum property

and sell it at a loss to private developers—the Federal Government making good two-thirds of the loss, and the city, one-third. The law did not stipulate the kind of construction to take place on such property. Moses thus saw Title I as providing the site of a new opera house. He offered a slum area at Columbus Circle but insisted that the Metropolitan Opera Board pledge a million dollars to prove their intention to build. John D. Rockefeller, Jr., quickly pledged half that amount. But then Moses heard that the Chairman of the Board of the Metropolitan Opera had said, "Well, after all, the new opera house is nothing more than a dream..."

"It's all off," Moses exploded. "The offer is withdrawn."

But he had been bitten by a big idea, and it stayed with him. In the course of the coming years, Moses offered the Metropolitan Opera a variety of sites, ranging from an area in Washington Square to an old trolley-car barn on Third Avenue. All were seriously considered and regretfully refused. Then, one day, a new idea emerged.

Robert Blum, head of the Brooklyn Institute of Arts and Letters and an old friend of Moses, was sharing a cab with him on the way to an appointment. As they passed a slum area in the west Sixties, called Lincoln Square, Blum remembers, Moses said to him, "Someday we've got to do something about that slum."

The time soon came. Moses offered the Lincoln Square tract to the Met but now insisted they raise one and a half million dollars towards land cost within six weeks. "And this time I don't want any more backfires."

The thirty members of the Metropolitan Opera Board drove to Lincoln Square to see what they would get. It was a badly blighted thirteen-block area packed with 5,400 families, primarily Puerto Rican—certainly one of the most congested areas in the city.

Long, long ago, the area had been "a sweet rural valley, beautiful with man a bright flower, refreshed by man a pure streamlet, and enlivened here and there by a delectable Little Dutch cottage, sheltered under some sloping hill; and almost buried in embowering trees." That was in the middle of the 1600's when the Dutch plows broke the plains and called the place "Bloemendael,"

which meant "vale of flowers." Bloemendael became Bloomingdale, a section of graceful summer homes where country squires bred horses, hunted bear and fox and wolves, fished the streamlets of the Great Kill River which ran through the area, and brought home huge lobsters, giant oysters and sturgeon from the nearby Hudson River.

The first dramatic change came with the American Revolution. Some of the largest land-owners loaned out their homes to headquarter the Hessian troops, and the vengeful patriots burned the houses to the ground. After the war John Somerindyke bought most of the land at auction, and soon the area was again dotted with the splendid mansions of the Beekmans, the Bayers, the de Peysters, the Van de Heuvels, the Dyck-manns, the Cuttings, the Clendinings, and the Wells—the leading families of New York. Louis Philippe, future King of France, was a frequent guest of Somerindyke, and Mme. D'Auliffee, Marie Antoinette's lady-in-waiting, had a house here, as did the American mistress of Joseph Bonaparte.

Bloomingdale changed again when a road was cut through it connecting Gramercy Park to Harlem Heights. It was then a country drive "of unsurpassed beauty, up hill and down dale, varied with many a curve, and, at short intervals, enlivened by an enchanting view of the Hudson." Burnham's Tavern, where Lincoln Center now stands, was a favorite stopping place for driving parties in elegant carriages. But with the road came more people, and then more homes. Soon there was a stoneyard on the river bank and the woodcutters moved in. George Pope Morris gave a woodcutter ten dollars to spare a beautiful old elm, then wrote his famous poem, "Woodman Spare That Tree." Edgar Allan Poe lived nearby and wrote "The Raven" there.

Bloomingdale Drive became "The Boulevard" after the Civil War, "divided for its full length by a strip of green flanked on each side by trees." The New York *Tribune* called it "the only street that does not depend on the buildings for its beauty." But just before the turn of the century, the Boulevard became "Broadway," a considerably widened road, and farmhouses became road-

houses and restaurants and beer-gardens. The wealthy moved away onto the strips along the park and the river, and the area's genteel history was over.

First came the squatters and then the speculators. They used the cheap, local brown stone to put up rows and rows of identical houses, jammed next to each other. Their only individuality lay in ornamented facades, cornices, gables, dormers, bay windows. Many of these homes were soon converted into rooming houses, divided and sub-divided as the people kept coming.

In a massive effort to rejuvenate the area, the fabulous Century Theater was constructed on Central Park West, only a block away from where Lincoln Center now stands. A spectacular place, with a horseshoe of ornate boxes for its patrons, the Century was an attempt at creating a national theater. New Yorkers, however, soon dubbed it "The Shrine of Snobbery," and it quickly failed, despite the fact that Florenz Ziegfeld produced some of his famous musicals there.

On the adjoining streets, just outside the growing Lincoln Square slum, an expanding colony of writers, artists, musicians and actors emerged. They had their own colorful restaurants such as the Irish Emerald Lunch, their own social clubs, a gym run by the Reilly family, a news-stand operated by a former pianist and artist who were then blind. The Twelfth Regiment Armory, located in the area, was used as background for many motion pictures having a medieval theme. The nearby Columbia Storage Warehouse became the repository for artifacts of a young theatrical heritage. In the New Deal days, the Works Progress Administration had its city headquarters in a loft building right in the heart of Lincoln Square. During much of the Depression, the WPA served as the sole hope for hundreds of people in the arts, and out of the group came some of the exciting talent of our time.

The visiting Board members of the Metropolitan Opera knew little of this history. They saw Lincoln Square for what it then was: a slum area full of broken-down buildings, crawling with rats and roaches, and packed with the poor. Yet despite that, a majority of the Board voted to raise money to explore the area's potential. Major credit for the decision goes to three men: Charles Spofford, Irving Olds and C. D. Jackson. Olds was the retired Chairman of the Board of U. S. Steel and had the quiet force of authority that came with that background; C. D. Jackson was the brash, energetic publisher of *Fortune* magazine.

For almost a decade, Wallace K. Harrison had been the architectural consultant for the Metropolitan Opera House. He has been variously described as an architectural tycoon, a modernist, a reactionary, a maverick (his own description), a tough construction man, a gentle-hearted aesthete and the most powerful and influential of America's 22,000 registered architects. Harrison is a major proponent of the so-called "slab," or glass block on end. He had been involved with the planning of Rockefeller Center and once, in defending his view, told John D. Rockefeller, Jr., "Dammit, Mr. Rockefeller, you can't *do* that! You'll ruin the building if you cover up its lines with classical gingerbread!" As chief architect of the United Nations, Harrison supervised the work of some of the world's great designers from France, Belgium, China, Sweden, Russia and England.

Harrison had large files of preliminary sketches for a new opera house that he had been considering for more than ten years, but now he started afresh for the proposed new site.

Then came the "grand coincidence."

The New York Philharmonic Orchestra had recently been notified that their Carnegie Hall lease would be canceled and they had three years to find a new home. Once before they had asked Harrison to draw sketches for a new hall just north of Rockefeller Center, but the plan never materialized. It was Harrison who now suggested to Arthur Houghton, President of the New York Philharmonic, that the Met and the Philharmonic might get together on a combined concept for a new home.

Arthur Houghton is another strong man with a decisive mind. Among other things, he was President of Steuben Glass, President of the English-Speaking Union, trustee of the Metropolitan Museum of Art, The New York Public Library and the Rockefeller Foundation.

Harrison's idea intrigued Houghton enough to set up a meeting on Randall's Island with Moses and Spofford. The meeting went well. "I remember coming back over the Triborough Bridge in a taxi with Arthur and Wally," said Spofford, "and Arthur was saying, 'Well, there may very well be something in this. Why don't we talk about it some more?' "

They had dinner at the Knickerbocker Club and Harrison presented a vision of a single building with a great common foyer and two separate halls. Out of this group's excitement came the formation of a Joint Exploratory Committee made up of members from both the Met and the Philharmonic. It soon became obvious, however, that there was a serious void. A chairman was needed, a man of national distinction and neutral views but a man of undisputed strength. The Dukes needed a Prince.

One of the men at that first Exploratory Committee meeting was Anthony Bliss, a member of the Met Board, as his father had been. It was the senior Bliss who had helped buy the stock of the old Metropolitan Opera House from the real estate company that owned it. That company consisted of box-holders of the so-called Diamond Horseshoe who had grown increasingly skeptical about their involvement in a deficit operation. In his father's files Anthony Bliss found folders dating back to 1917 that were marked NEW OPERA HOUSE. There was even a plan for an art center to include a new opera house, concert hall, theater and school. It was one of his father's unfulfilled dreams and now Bliss helped it become realized.

After the first meeting of the Exploratory Committee, Bliss explained, "I heard by chance that night that John Rockefeller had just finished a major job in philanthropy and was looking for another important civic project that might interest him. I remember calling up Chuck Spofford and telling him I'd heard this. And Chuck said, 'Well, that's fine, because I'm dining with him over the weekend and I'll sound him out.' "

Spofford and Rockefeller were members of a Council on Foreign Relations study group that had scheduled a meeting in the Poconos to discuss Russia. "Between the sessions," Spofford remem-

bers, "John and I sat out on a bench and I told him about the thing, and what I thought it might mean for the cultural life of the city and the country. I told him I thought it was a really big project."

John D. Rockefeller 3rd was born and bred into the idea of the "big project." His grandfather, John Davison Rockefeller, Sr., was known in his lifetime as the richest man in the world. John D. Rockefeller, Jr., an only son, became one of the leading philanthropists in the United States and set up the Rockefeller Foundation, a fountainhead of funds for many of the world's worthy causes. "Mister Junior," as he was called, also organized the Rockefeller Institute for Medical Research, built Rockefeller Center, reconstructed the Cloisters in Ft. Tryon Park, donated land for the United Nations headquarters and financed low-cost housing all over the city.

John D. Rockefeller 3rd ("Mr. John"), eldest of five sons of "Mister Junior," is a quiet-spoken, courtly man with a quick, broad-ranging mind and a strong will. He not only is former President of the Rockefeller Brothers Fund and serves now as Chairman of the Rockefeller Foundation, but he has also founded the Asia Society, the Agricultural Development Council and the Population Council. At the time Spofford spoke to him about the new Center, most of Rockefeller's time and interest had been concentrated in the international area.

"What caught me was the real need of the Center and my deep feeling that I ought to think more seriously of my responsibilities as a citizen of New York," Rockefeller said. "But besides that, there was the fascination of the three coincidences. There was the Metropolitan's decision to move, the Philharmonic's need for a new home and the availability of land in Lincoln Square."

As the new chairman, Rockefeller quickly put the Exploratory Committee into high gear. First, he invited several key men to join the committee.

Having been involved with a great many projects he was adept at the delicate art of choosing the people to make a project move. The real leader knows that most of the people who have time and are looking for something to do are often not very helpful—they're usually earnest people but not fighters, drivers, doers. The

men Rockefeller wanted were the busy men with a record of success and a broad range of contacts.

"It's a strange thing," Rockefeller commented, "but in all the many things I've seen happen, there are always only a half dozen people who truly make it happen—no matter how big the thing is, it's often the same few people who make it happen."

One of these people was Devereux C. Josephs, then Chairman of the Board of the New York Life Insurance Company. "I was determined not to join anything else because I was really busy," remarked the soft-spoken Josephs, his gentle face smiling at the memory. "But when John Rockefeller and Charles Spofford came to my office and said, 'This is an idea we have,' it seemed such an exciting thing to do that I tore up my resolutions and joined up. Besides," he added, "I was very fond of these two individuals—we had done other things together."

The three men had worked on the Council on Foreign Relations and Josephs and Rockefeller also had served together on the United Negro College Fund.

Rockefeller next approached Robert Blum, head of the Brooklyn Institute of Arts and Letters, of which the Brooklyn Academy of Music was part. Rockefeller also had worked with Blum on a variety of projects and respected his background in cultural affairs. More than that, Rockefeller wanted Blum to serve as liaison with Robert Moses, as well as with various city agencies.

Rockefeller now described the project as "a venture in faith." He was determined to give it much more than his money and the magnetism of his name—he was convinced that this project was worthy of his fullest understanding and time, and that the challenge of this project might well be one of the big things in his life.

It was true that he had little background in the arts. It was also true that he had only scant knowledge of architecture and construction. But he knew how to listen and learn, and, most important, he knew how to lead.

Rockefeller set up a regular series of luncheon meetings, every second Monday at the Century Club, always in the same room at the same hour. The participants were among the busiest, most important men in New York, but few were ever late, and fewer were ever absent.

It was a compact group: Chairman Rockefeller; Spofford, Jackson and Olds representing the Metropolitan Opera; Houghton, David Keiser, and at the beginning, Floyd Blair, representing the Philharmonic; Lincoln Kirstein of the New York City Ballet; architect Wallace Harrison; as well as Josephs, Blum, and Anthony Bliss, ex-officio. Rockefeller insisted that meetings start promptly at 12:30, and they did.

"We didn't wait for food; business started right away," said Blum. "The Chairman never could eat much lunch, but the others did."

"People are always asking what goes on at meetings like this," Josephs remarked. "They think it's some kind of mysterious, arcane, esoteric conversation that goes on with a lot of wise people. Not at all: They eat their soup noisily, and they listen, and sometimes at the end they come up with something that's pretty intelligent. Sometimes they speak without thinking. Lots of people think while they're speaking. Sometimes they'll spark somebody's idea, and then something may happen. The emphasis is on action rather than argument, and there is minimal time available for anything petty."

These were people with a common goal. There was a great deal of discussion, but conversations moved quickly.

"The tone of the meetings? Generally serious, but not mournful," said Arthur Houghton. "There was a lot of good humor and some flashes of real wit. We were a very compatible group of men. Before we were finished, we all knew each other very well. One of the most important things about this group is that they were all flexible."

Their primary job was to develop a set of principles and a plan. They were not as much concerned with details as with experts. Part of their job was to pick the creative brains of the country. In doing so, they found themselves enlarging their original concept. The committee soon grew into a Board of Directors.

"We had some wonderful, extravagant brainstorming sessions," added Houghton. "We would sit around and say, 'Well, if we're going to have the Opera and we're going to have the Philhar-

monic, why not have the Ballet?' Everybody agreed. 'And why not have a theater, and why not have this and why not have that?' We even went into the possibility of including the visual arts, but then we realized that this seemed to be going a little too far because we already had some excellent art museums scattered all over the city. But we tossed everything into these original discussions, just to make sure we overlooked nothing."

There were a great many subcommittee sessions on a vast variety of subjects, engaging the most prominent experts in each field. Anthony Bliss remembered one session about music as having lasted several days, with Aaron Copland and other musicians and critics debating what Lincoln Center should be from the ideal musical standpoint. Board member David Keiser figured prominently in many of the music discussions since he himself was an accomplished pianist, a Juilliard graduate and a Director of Juilliard. Chairman of the Board of several sugar companies, Keiser also became President of the New York Philharmonic. On the Lincoln Center Board he was known as a quiet man with an easy smile and a decisive mind.

Basically, however, the Lincoln Center Board was a group of nonprofessionals constantly tapping the minds and talents of the top professionals in the country. "They would then sift all these collected ideas into the integrated concept," said Keiser, "but they were the ones who did the sifting."

One of the professionals invited to discuss the educational potential of Lincoln Center was Dr. George D. Stoddard, who was then Chancellor and Executive Vice President of New York University. He also had served as President of the University of the State of New York, Commissioner of Education and President of the University of Illinois. In his spare time, he was on the Board of the American Shakespeare Festival Theater and of the National Educational Television and Radio Center. Asked for his views, Stoddard told the Board bluntly, "Lincoln Center must not be a sort of Golden Horseshoe for a few special people. Lincoln Center should be part of the educational and cultural experience of the young people." After the prolonged questioning period, Stoddard told another invited guest, "I don't suppose we'll be asked in again, because we didn't offer anything except some obligations." But the Board promptly put Stoddard in charge of a Committee on Creative Arts and Education, a job that lasted more than ten years.

As the Lincoln Center concept was expanded—and soon they were talking about a music school, a library and even a museum—one question was constantly raised: "Where are we going to get the money?"

Money did not seem a desperate problem at the time because all these men were accustomed to financial dealings. They knew where the money was and how to get it. Furthermore, the Rockefeller name was an enormous asset in any fund-raising, for this was the third generation of Rockefeller philanthropy. It was only reasonable to expect that any Rockefeller-sponsored cause would get a warm reception from a vast number of people and institutions.

Still, the original concept had grown into a monumental idea requiring many millions of dollars. The Exploratory Committee had firmly decided that a center for the Performing Arts was not only feasible, but desirable—and a corporation should be formed to raise the money to build the place.

That, more than anything else, is what the concept had become: a sense of place. Grouping the units together not only created a dramatic idea that would facilitate fund-raising, but it was hoped that interaction among the units would create artistic dynamism.

There were many critics of the entire concept. Robert Brustein wrote in *The New Republic*, "You cannot create a cultural center unless you have first created a culture."

"Oh, that's nonsense," countered Devereux Josephs. "They grow together! Culture creates the surroundings, and the surroundings create the culture. They go hand-in-glove."

But the time had come to firm the shape of the hand.

What about the culture of the rest of the world? John D. Rockefeller 3rd, together with Anthony Bliss and architect Wallace Harrison,

took a tour of fourteen cities in eight countries in Europe, talking with leading experts in the performing arts, visiting their theaters and schools, picking up ideas. The chandelier in the new Metropolitan Opera House that dramatically pulls up at the start of a performance is the result of something that Harrison saw in a small, beautiful theater in Munich. And one of the people who most impressed the Rockefeller group with his imaginative concept of drama training was Michel Saint-Denis, in Strasbourg, who was later brought in to advise on drama training at the new Juilliard School.

It was a profitable trip, but with a serious limitation: They could pick up parts and pieces of an artistic mosaic for future use, but there was no mural to duplicate. The closest counterpart was a grouping of cultural buildings in Brussels, but that had no central core, no overall operation.

A core was the unique element of the Lincoln Center concept and the most difficult to distill. After all, the Metropolitan Opera and the New York Philharmonic were both units of great reputation and impressive history, and each had a natural instinct to maintain its individual identity. It would be difficult to surrender some of that individuality to the larger concept of a Lincoln Center for the Performing Arts. It took patient persuasion by the Lincoln Center Board to sell the idea that Lincoln Center must not simply be a landlord, it must itself be a hub.

John Rockefeller 3rd raised another question: If Lincoln Center was supposed to represent the finest in American performing arts, wasn't the New York City Center entitled to a place? At first, the idea seemed contradictory. City Center had a long-term home in the old Mecca Temple and annually presented its own theater, opera, and ballet season. So initially City Center was not even interested. They became interested as they recognized the potential benefits of a new, permanent home equipped with the most modern facilities. The idea was complicated, however, by the thought of having two opera companies in a single center, perhaps even performing the same opera on the same night. But, it was argued, their audiences would be different, as would their price scales. When it came to making a final decision, all this was discussed, and the Metropolitan Opera agreed to the admission of City Center with all its units. More than anything else, that decision demonstrated that Lincoln Center as a whole was to be greater than any of its parts.

The question of a repertory theater was also a difficult one: Should Lincoln Center invite in an established company, or should it set up its own? Repertory theater has had a rocky history throughout this country, and the Board could not agree that there then existed a single outstanding repertory company. The decision, therefore, was that Lincoln Center should start its own.

And what about a library, and a museum? Back in June 1917, Oscar Sanick, Chief of the Library of Congress Music Division, had written in *Art World* that someday we must have museums of music. "A fantastic dream? Not at all!" wrote Sanick. Dr. Carleton Sprague Smith remembered Sanick's article and in 1931 developed from it the idea of a "Library-Museum of the Performing Arts."

For this concept, too, there was neither prototype nor parallel anywhere in the world. Fortunately Dr. Smith had support for the project from The New York Public Library—Smith served on its Board of Directors. Other Public Library Board members included Arthur Houghton, Devereux Josephs and Irving Olds. Smith was also on the Board of the Metropolitan and the Philharmonic, just as many of the other men were on several Boards. Again, it was the overlapping of their serving several institutions that helped enlarge the concept of Lincoln Center.

Finally to be dealt with was the need for an educational institution within the new cultural family. Juilliard School of Music was one of the more likely candidates. Juilliard was both distinctive and distinguished, and it was at a crossroads. There was an internal struggle: whether to remain small and select or to grow nationally and start a branch school in Los Angeles.

President of Juilliard at that time was William Schuman, a gifted musician in his own right. John Erskine once described Schuman as "a radical with a conservative manner," meaning that Schuman was a man with an organized and practical mind who had ideas and imagination beyond the framework of an ordinary director.

Schuman invited Rockefeller and the Lincoln Center leaders to attend a Juilliard Board meeting. That meeting stirred up a mutual excitement. Juilliard agreed to expand its school to include drama, and the union was accomplished.

And so there it was: The concept now had both a framework and a family.

The next need was money, more money than had ever been raised for any cultural project in our country's history. Here's how impossible the dream was: The last huge sum attempted for culture in this country was a projected $3 million for the Metropolitan Opera—and that had not been fully realized. Here now was an engineering firm estimating a budget for Lincoln Center at $75 million ($55 million for buildings and $20 million for the triple purpose of a building contingency, an education or scholarship fund and a fund for creative advancement). It seemed an absurd expectation (and it was actually less than half the total finally needed).

But our country was changing. More people had leisure and money than ever before. Even in 1957 America had at least 80 opera companies, close to 1,000 symphony orchestras, and some 5,000 community theaters. Every fourth phonograph record sold was of classical music, and, unbelievable though it seemed, paid admissions to concerts exceeded those of baseball games by more than $5 million every year.

Fund-raising, however, needs professionals. Kersting, Brown & Co. was brought in because they had raised millions of dollars for some of the country's largest colleges. For their campaign manager, John Rockefeller and Irving Olds went to see Clarence Francis, Chairman of the Board of General Foods. They were all old friends, and Francis listened respectfully, then said, "I'm 69 years old, and any idea of getting me to do this thing now is utterly ridiculous. Go and get yourself a young man who's in business today, and functioning."

Rockefeller and Olds, however, returned a second time, then a third time and finally Francis

said, "Well, if you can't get anyone else, I guess you've got me."

What had attracted Francis was the same thing that had intrigued all these busy men: the challenge.

"New York City was just No-Man's-Land as far as its cultural reputation was concerned," said Francis. "Most visitors simply saw New York as a financial institution—it was profits, it was money, money, money. And this was wrong. The thing that fascinated me was that New York now could be made the cultural center of the world. That was it completely; that it would give to New York and the country something else, something that would be the seed to start things going in other places all over the country and the world."

A tall, silver-haired, friendly man, Clarence Francis says of himself, "I've been a prune peddler all my life." Since General Foods is one of the giant foods companies in the country, that seems a slight simplification. Francis was also one of those who helped form the Committee of Economic Development and the Nutritional Institute, both large money-raising projects.

Working as a team, Rockefeller and Francis went, almost literally, ringing doorbells. But they went where the money was to be found—to the heads of the largest corporations in the country. No one had ever gone to big business for big money to support the arts. "And without John D. Rockefeller," said Francis, "I don't think it ever could have been done. I've never kidded myself on that."

Francis usually began by telling the company president: "Listen, we came to you as chief executive for one simple reason. We know you have a policy of not giving money for this. That policy has to be changed and you're the man to change it."

"John would usually let me start the interview," he said. "He'd sit back, listening and watching. And if he thought that something I said just didn't hit right, he'd come in. And if he ever started to talk, believe me, I let him talk."

Often the company president would listen carefully, then say, "John, you really *do* believe in this?" And Rockefeller would answer, "Yes, I *do*

believe in it. I believe it is important for our city. I believe it is important for our country. I believe it is important for the world."

After that, the usual question was, "How much do you want?"

"And we would tell them," Francis continued. "We had it pretty well figured out; and we let them know we weren't after chickenfeed. Another thing: It was a capital contribution not to be repeated. They were not obligating themselves to give more in the future."

Of course, it didn't work out that way. The initial budget estimate for Lincoln Center was too low, and it had to be raised several times. So Francis and Rockefeller did find themselves making repeat trips to the same big contributors.

"You simply had to be honest and say to them, 'Look, if you think I'm not more humiliated than you, you're crazy.'" But then Francis would add, "We're building something for the ages. We're building a cultural center. We're building something that will be here for 500 years. This must be done right."

Francis is an exuberant man, and Rockefeller often acted as his keel. "John was quiet but firm," Francis remarked. "I once had the idea of making Lincoln Center fund-raising a national proposition, getting every state in the union in back of it. I envisioned it as a national expression of culture, with each state recognized in it. But Rockefeller said, 'No, I think it would be better if the state money served as seed money for their own local cultural projects.'

"I could see his point," said Francis, "and I got the message. When I say positive, John is."

What Rockefeller and his Board knew was that any cultural project is almost automatically a deficit operation. The Lincoln Center Board therefore decided that they must build Lincoln Center *without* a mortgage. They would not saddle any future center with a building bondage to add to its anticipated deficit. That was an admirable proposal but almost unheard of, particularly in view of the amount of money it suggested.

The professional fund-raisers, Kersting, Brown & Co., started from scratch with a single file of several hundred names of people previously involved with New York City's cultural organizations, particularly the Metropolitan Opera and the Philharmonic. This initial filebox soon grew into a cabinet with some ten thousand names, a carefully culled list: sponsors of previous music festivals, wealthy friends of Board members, any foundation that had a music-related interest, people mentioned in magazine articles. Someone was even put to work tracing genealogies to check if any member of a wealthy family had an obvious interest in the performing arts.

The initial handful of fund-raisers gradually grew into a highly organized group of about 5,000 people. The single committee of two dozen top community leaders had multiplied into dozens and dozens of committees of all kinds—committees for women, for suburbanites, for businessmen. Committee members were always going to teas, always making speeches, always showing artists' renderings of how the Center might finally look.

The walls of the central campaign office served as a bulletin board for the various committee members, who checked them regularly for names of potential major contributors. "I know him; I'll go see him," one might say, and then initial the name, take a campaign kit with literature and pledge cards and go off to seek a contribution. George Moore, then Vice President of the First National City Bank and Chairman of the Patron Committee, would never ask for less than $100,000, "and" he then remarked, "I won't ask if I think I'm going to get No for an answer." Those giving to the patron program were told they would have their names carved in marble on the site and would have the VIP privilege of watching rehearsals from a private viewing room.

Big money also came in from foundations (the Ford Foundation gave $25 million) and from foreign governments. The German cultural attaché, for example, met with Clarence Francis, who indicated how nice a gesture it would be if the Germans contributed, and so they did. The Rockefeller family had been deeply involved in helping varied groups in Japan, so Japanese business circles decided to reciprocate by contributing to Lincoln Center. And C. D. Jackson suggested to the Italian Ambassador that it would

indeed be friendly of Italy to contribute Roman travertine marble for the exterior of one of the buildings; Rockefeller wrote a follow-up letter that firmed the agreement. It was a kind of international cooperation that nobody had ever tried before.

"There's a time for John to step in," said Francis, "and he steps in beautifully."

Rockefeller stepped in again to help get city, state and federal funds, without which final completion of the venture would not have been possible. Federal money, of course, already was deep into the project through the Slum Clearance Law. City money was involved with a public garage for the Center and an outdoor concert area called Damrosch Park. State money arrived as a result of a unique Lincoln Center proposal to Governor Nelson Rockefeller: "Why spend a lot of money at Flushing Meadows for cultural aspects at the New York World's Fair, when New York State can build a permanent building right in Lincoln Center?"

This appealed to Governor Rockefeller, who didn't want to construct a building at the Fair that would simply become another ice-skating rink—as did the state building at the previous New York Fair. Out of that combined thinking, plus some pivotal pressure from John D. Rockefeller, came the funds—from the state and city—to build the State Theater and the Library & Museum.

With the site established and the funds available, focus now shifted to the architects. They were six of America's most prominent architects— six notable temperaments, each with his own distinct ideas about design and aesthetics. Besides Harrison there was his partner, Max Abramovitz, who would design Philharmonic Hall; Philip Johnson, the State Theater; Gordon Bunshaft (representing Skidmore, Owings and Merrill), doing the Library-Museum; Eero Saarinen, the Repertory Theater; and Pietro Belluschi, Dean of Architecture at the Massachusetts Institute of Technology, The Juilliard School.

All of them had originally been trained in the principles of the International School—believing that form follows function; that space is enclosed by thin planes of surfaces, rather than solidity;

that the emphasis is on interior volume, not exterior mass; that forms are generally geometric with large glass areas.

"The six of us may have had different ideas," said Philip Johnson, "but after all, we were on the same side of the fence. We all came up through the Modern Movement together, and we were all looking away now from the puritanism of the International style toward enriched forms."

First, though, came the preliminaries: the "planning book" that provides a base for the work by detailing the size of the property, location of traffic, directions of streets, zoning limitations, etc. "Then you start trying to find out what the demands are for the buildings and match the two," said Harrison.

The six architects had regular luncheon meetings at Harrison's office, and the sessions always stretched late into the afternoon. There were the early big questions: Do we have a closed concept or an open concept? Should there be a great wall, high and solid, to keep the city noises out—a controlled space which is entered through a grand door? Or should it be open to let the city flow freely into and out of the area? Do we have one building, or do we group several buildings together? Should there be a large, open forecourt or a short one to allow immediate access to a building? Should there be a balanced, formal scheme for placing the buildings, or should it be more informal and free? Should any one building be dominant?

"We all worked for about a year on general schemes, working out the locations and the way the buildings were to front in relation to the city and what we could afford to do about traffic," Harrison explained.

"You sort of negotiated things," Gordon Bunshaft commented. "There just wasn't anybody saying, 'It's going to be like this!' Nobody was in a position to dictate that."

"None of us was big enough to say, 'Pick one of us!'" said Philip Johnson, "so it was like six poets trying to write a poem."

"The one-architect idea never came out," said quiet, thoughtful Max Abramovitz. "You can do that with a hundred-million-dollar office building because there's a lot of routine stuff that serves one idea. But here you had six special buildings, and each Board of each unit wanted its own personal attention from its own architect. It made me think of the way the United States must have been when it was thirteen states and they tried to make it into one country. Each architect, like each state, is jealous and afraid that the other one would dominate him. It took a lot of time and give-and-take to fuse the concept. We all had to cross-recognize each other; and we all had to compromise."

Again, it was John D. Rockefeller 3rd who stepped in, both as client and arbitrator. His was the rare gift of quiet persuasion. He wouldn't force an idea, but he had the subtle knack of bringing a discussion back to the critical points and putting it all into perspective.

"We were just six guys talking to the wind, until John came in as the referee," said Bunshaft, who himself is strong-minded and emphatic.

"We got involved in whether they would be closed buildings or open buildings," Abramovitz recalled. "And I built up a strong argument for having glassy, open buildings, and a day-and-night thing. And Rockefeller told the others, 'All right, he's going to start. And I don't want him to start unless all of you will accept the overall concept and the scale, and once you accept it, go along with it, so that we have unity.'"

When Belluschi's plan for Juilliard became larger than expected and the space situation became tighter and tighter, it was General Otto Nelson who figured out a way to get more land. A top engineer, Nelson was in charge of Lincoln Center construction. He persuaded Washington officials to condemn more slumland on a half-block area between 65th and 66th streets, just across from Lincoln Center's three-block area. Juilliard was to be moved there and Belluschi was pleased. He said simply, "We hang together or we hang separately."

The one piece of land the architects could not maneuver was the park and bandshell area that Robert Moses had set for the southwest corner of Lincoln Center. Moses refused to have that site changed.

"The decision to chop off one corner for that park really stopped us," said Bunshaft. "If we could have had the freedom to move it around, we probably would have come up with a much more exciting master plan."

The time finally came for large-scale plasticine models. The architects wrapped themselves in towels to keep their clothes clean and used their pencils to move buildings around, group, separate and regroup. One of the men purposefully sliced off the top of the model State Theater. Philip Johnson glowered, walked away from it, and returned, but the top never went on again. More buildings were sliced up, some were redesigned from scratch. The prime question always remained: Does any specific building interfere with someone's notion of the total aesthetic scheme? However cautious this questioning, several of the architects felt that they were all involved in a kind of tug-of-war, each man subtly maneuvering for more space, each unconsciously determined to build a monument to himself.

As the architects were settling into general agreement about design a large human problem was still unresolved. Although the site for the new Center was a blighted neighborhood that had been set for renewal, it was still a neighborhood. More than 5,000 families lived there and nearly 600 small businesses were in the area. The questions were: Where could they go? What would they do? And who cared enough to do something?

At the public hearings before the City Planning Commission, the debate was open and heated. People wore small badges saying FOR or AGAINST. Rockefeller spoke earnestly of the two years spent in studying the project and called it "a truly great civic development for the benefit and enjoyment of all its people." William Schuman talked of the union of kindred arts in a single center where each can gain from the other, "where one artist can inspire another . . . where one art form can complement another. . . ."

And one speaker made the point that the people living on the site would be properly taken care of, that all the problems would be resolved satisfactorily because the Lincoln Center Board of Directors "are men accustomed to success."

They were indeed. On that cold winter day when Lincoln Center took legal possession of the area, oil and coal trucks checked all 526 buildings, and teams of contractors made basic repairs. A responsible firm of relocation agents had been hired to find improved accommodations for the neighborhood families. All moving expenses were reimbursed, and the families who made their own move got bonuses up to $500. As soon as a house became vacant, it was torn down.

There was only small sentiment for the slums. The first building to be razed was a typical four-and-a-half-story brownstone built in 1881, originally for a single family and servants. It had later become a rooming house of twelve apartments. As many as six persons lived in each one-and-a-half-room apartment, sharing a single bathroom with four other families. Rats and roaches infested the place. "The rats are so big," Mrs. Virginia Diaz had said, "I stay awake all night to keep them away from the baby."

The relocation took almost three years. Lincoln Center's ground-breaking ceremony was scheduled for May 14, 1959. President Dwight D. Eisenhower agreed to shovel up the first fresh dirt.

In charge of preparing the site for the ceremony was Colonel William F. Powers, former head of the U.S. Army Engineer District in Philadelphia and now assistant to Otto Nelson in charge of construction.

It rained steadily that week and Powers fervently hoped it would stop; though he had a tent over the bandstand, there was none for the audience. Still, on the appointed day, everything was ready on schedule, including the sunshine.

The program was carefully selected, with Leonard Bernstein acting as Master of Ceremonies and conducting Aaron Copland's *Fanfare*. The Juilliard chorus sang the National Anthem, and Risë Stevens, Juilliard graduate and noted mezzo-soprano of the Metropolitan Opera, sang an aria from *Carmen*.

Mayor Robert Wagner, Robert Moses and John D. Rockefeller 3rd all made brief speeches. Moses said, "Mr. Rockefeller and his associates still have a long way to go to their final magnificent objective, but no one who knows them, their motives, their reputation, their persistence, their pride in this city and their belief in the national

21

and international repercussions of the Performing Arts Center can have the slightest doubt of the outcome."

But after listening to the concert, President Eisenhower quipped to the audience, "If they can do this under a tent, why the Square?"

A few minutes later the President used a chrome-plated spade to dig up four shovelsful of grayish earth while the Juilliard chorus and the one hundred members of the New York Philhar-monic Orchestra launched into the Hallelujah chorus from Handel's *Messiah*.

Shortly afterward 44-year-old Anthony Capasso dug the bucket of his giant power shovel into the ground to begin actual construction of Lincoln Center for the Performing Arts.

The New York *Daily News* headlined its editorial: NOW LET'S GET ON WITH IT!

Rockefeller's "venture in faith" had really begun.

1

The need for funds is a continuing factor in the operation of Lincoln Center. (1) This Christmas greeting, featuring art work by *New Yorker* cartoonist B. Tobey, was sent out in 1961. The Consolidated Corporate Fund Drive was launched in 1970, (2) and a meeting of its steering committee is shown here. Members are (*left to right*) David M. Keiser; Mrs. Irving Mitchell Felt; Hoyt Ammidon, Chairman of the Fund Drive; Robert V. Lindsay; Amyas Ames, Chairman of the Board of Lincoln Center; John W. Mazzola; Frank S. Gilligan; Robert L. Hoguet; and Mrs. Lewis W. Douglas.

2

General information

Box Office Information *For ticket information on these and other Lincoln Center events send a stamped, self-addressed envelope to: (Name of theater) Box Office, Lincoln Center Plaza, Broadway at 64th Street, New York, N.Y. 10023.*

Tickets are also available for an additional 35¢ at nine special Lincoln Center box offices at Bloomingdale's, New York City and Bergen County; and Abraham & Straus, Huntington, Hempstead, Manhasset, Garden City, West Babylon, Smith Haven and Brooklyn.

Guided Tours, Visitors Services *Hour-and-a-quarter tours daily from 10 to 5 include usually Philharmonic Hall, New York State Theater, Vivian Beaumont Theater and Metropolitan Opera House (except Saturday). Occasionally a building may be excluded due to a special rehearsal or event. Adults $1.85. Students $1.25. Children $1.00. Reservations are required for groups of 10 or more.*

For further information, write or call: Visitors Services, Lincoln Center Plaza, B'way at 64th Street, New York, N.Y. 10023. TR 4-4010.

Lincoln Center *administrative offices, 1865 B'way, New York, N.Y. 10023. Phone 765-5100.*

Restaurants *Philharmonic Hall, Philharmonic Cafe, Plaza level. The Footlights Cafeteria, open daily 11:00 a.m. to 8:30 p.m., 140 W. 65th Street. Phone: TR 4-7000. New York State Theater, Promenade Cafe, Grand Promenade level. Beverages before and after performances, Metropolitan Opera House, The Opera Cafe, Plaza level. Open noon Monday through Saturday. Grand Tier, open two hours before performance for ticket holders only. Phone: 799-3400. Top of the Met: open to the public 5:30 to 8:00 p.m. Monday through Saturday; lunch Saturday 11:30 a.m. to 2:30 p.m. Reservations: 799-3737.*

Gift Shops *Philharmonic Hall. In lobby near the box office. Metropolitan Opera House, Publication Desk, Plaza level. Library & Museum. Sales Shop, Plaza level.*

How to Get to the Center *Subway: West Side IRT local, 66th St. station underground concourse to all buildings or IND trains to Columbus Circle, 59th St. station. Bus: The following bus lines stop at Lincoln Center: M-7—65th Street crosstown, M-104—Broadway line, 11—Amsterdam Avenue, 7—Broadway-Columbus Avenue, 5—Fifth Avenue-Riverside Drive, 6—72nd Street crosstown. Cars and taxis may enter a sheltered entrance-roadway at 64th St. and Amsterdam Ave. leaving passengers at the West Concourse with access to all theaters. Open from 11:00 a.m. to 1:00 p.m.*

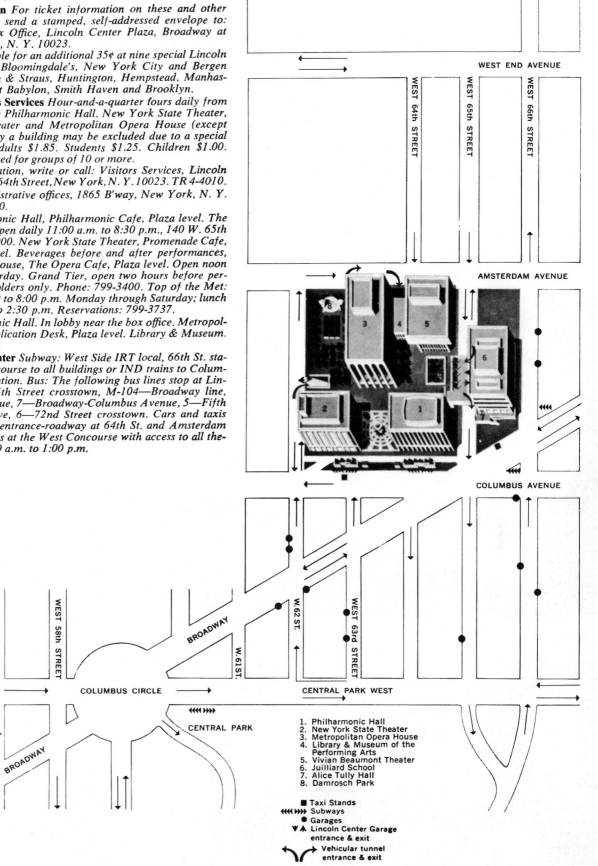

1. Philharmonic Hall
2. New York State Theater
3. Metropolitan Opera House
4. Library & Museum of the Performing Arts
5. Vivian Beaumont Theater
6. Juilliard School
7. Alice Tully Hall
8. Damrosch Park

■ Taxi Stands
◄◄◄ ►►► Subways
● Garages
▼ ▲ Lincoln Center Garage entrance & exit
Vehicular tunnel entrance & exit

A guide to Lincoln Center.

GUY GILLETTE

1

2

(1) An early model of Lincoln Center surrounded by outstanding personalities in the performing arts, from left: prima ballerina Alicia Markova; modern dance pioneer Martha Graham; composer, former President of The Juilliard School, and President Emeritus of Lincoln Center William Schuman; Juilliard student Dorothy Pixley; (*standing*) American soprano Lucine Amara; Director of the Metropolitan Opera, Rudolf Bing; Executive Director of Operations for the Center, Reginald Allen; Managing Director of the New York Philharmonic, George E. Judd, Jr.; composer, conductor, and Director of the New York Philharmonic, Leonard Bernstein; actress Julie Harris in costume for her role in *The Warm Peninsula*; and theatrical producer, Robert Whitehead.

(2) A biweekly luncheon meeting of the officers and Board of Directors for the planning of Lincoln Center.

(3) John D. Rockefeller 3rd making a point to Mayor Robert F. Wagner.

(4) At the historic ground-breaking ceremonies on May 14, 1959, President Dwight D. Eisenhower greets Mrs. Vivian Beaumont Allen (*center*), with Ambassador Richard Patterson and Mr. and Mrs. Rockefeller looking on. In the car is Mayor Robert F. Wagner.

(5) Architect Philip Johnson (*center*) inspects the pipes of the Plaza Fountain, which he designed.

3   BOB SERATING

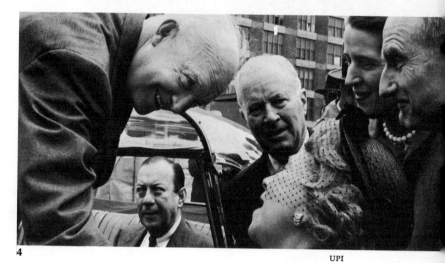

4   UPI

5   THE NEW YORK TIMES

1

(1) The ground-breaking ceremonies, May 14, 1959, with a crane waiting in the background.

(2) Painting by Lawrence M., 9 years old, on the theme of "What Lincoln Center Means to Me" for the Student Art Exhibit.

(3) Machinist Joseph Conifrey tends the crash helmet garden planted by construction workers at the Center site.

2

3

BOB SERATING   **2**   BOB SERATING   **3**   BOB SERATING   **4**

(1) John D. Rockefeller 3rd (*holding glasses*) shown on the model of three of the buildings—the New York State Theater, the Metropolitan Opera House, and Philharmonic Hall—with the Center's architects and designers, (*left to right*) Edward Mathews, Philip Johnson, Jo Mielziner, Wallace K. Harrison, the late Eero Saarinen, Gordon Bunshaft, Max Abramovitz, and Pietro Belluschi.

Some of the people who have been closely associated with operating Lincoln Center: (2) William Schuman, President Emeritus; Devereux C. Josephs; and Amyas Ames, Chairman of the Board; (3) Charles M. Spofford, Vice Chairman; (4) Lawrence A. Wien, Vice Chairman; (5) Clarence Francis; John D. Rockefeller 3rd, past Chairman; and Mrs. Rockefeller; (6) Hoyt Ammidon, Chairman of the Lincoln Center Fund and The Consolidated Corporate Fund Drive.

1

THE NEW YORK TIMES   1

GEORGE ANCONA   2

(1) Lincoln Center as seen from Broadway.

(2) Schoolchildren at Lincoln Center.

(3) The New York City retail business salutes Lincoln Center, this in the window of the Takashimaya shop on behalf of Japan.

JAPAN CONGRATULATES
NEW YORK CITY

FOR AN OUTSTANDING
CULTURAL ACHIEVEMENT.
...THE LINCOLN CENTER
FOR THE PERFORMING ARTS

Takashimaya

the
new york
philharmonic

"And so, on the 125th Anniversary, let us take deep satisfaction in the New York Philharmonic—not because it is one of the oldest orchestras in the world; not because it plays to one of the most sophisticated audiences of the world in one of the handsomest settings in the world; not because it is glamour personified; but because it is a national treasure. . . ."
—William Schuman

How do you house a national treasure? For this one, the shape and size of the house was secondary to the sound inside it. What was most wanted was a magnificent music box—"the finest musical instrument in America."

Architectural Forum offered some advice: "If you are building a concert hall and want instant acceptance, make it just like the one that was there before. . . . If you seek to improve on the past, prepare to suffer. But after people have gotten used to the new musical experience, you may wind up with one of the world's great concert halls."

The New York Philharmonic had had many homes since its founder Ureli Corelli Hill conducted the first concert on December 7, 1842, in the fashionable Apollo Rooms on lower Broadway. There followed the Assembly Rooms of the Chinese Building, Niblo's Concert Room, the Broadway Tabernacle, Steinway Hall, and then, many homes later, Carnegie Hall—where it stayed from 1892 to 1962.

The Philharmonic's ties to Carnegie were strong and sentimental. To the bravos of the world, it had performed in Carnegie Hall with most of the great conductors including Gustav Mahler, Arturo Toscanini, Dimitri Mitropoulos, Bruno Walter and Leonard Bernstein. The hall had been the mecca for many of the world's most celebrated composers: Dvořák, Rubinstein, Ravel, Strauss, Stravinsky, Copland. But now the lease at Carnegie was almost up, and time was running out. The Philharmonic needed a new home, a permanent home.

What about the sound of the proposed new hall?

"I remember very well when an acoustical expert asked one of our conductors what kind of sound he wanted in our hall," said David Keiser, then President of the New York Philharmonic. "The conductor answered, 'I want an ennobling sound,' and the expert just threw up his hands." Acoustical experts are not musicians. They talk in terms of decibels and cubic volume and reverberations.

"We talked to a large number of conductors," continued Keiser, "and we asked them two questions: 'Which concert hall do you think is the best in America, and which one is the best in Europe?' Their answers were almost unanimous: the *Grosser Musikverreinsaal* in Vienna and Boston's Symphony Hall [which was modeled after the *Gewandhaus* at the University of Leipzig]."

This gave the acousticians something specific to measure. They made binaural recordings and dimensional tabulations and materials analyses, testing the two halls for onstage blending, freedom from echo, and tonal balance. And they did this with some thirty other halls in fifteen countries.

Their critical test was for reverberation time—the length of time a sound lingers in the hall after its source has stopped. If the reverberation time is too short (less than 1.5 seconds), the sound seems dry and dead. If the time is 1.7 to 1.9 seconds, the music takes on an aliveness and a power. But if the reverberation time is too long, the sounds jostle each other and the tone flow becomes blurred and confused. The speaking voice is best heard in rooms of short reverberation time, while organ and choral music require longer reverberation. To incease the reverberation time, the volume of the hall must be increased; to decrease it requires more sound-absorption surfaces.

All these tests and statistics were fed into a computer, and out came the measurements of the optimum concert hall: a cubic volume between 500,000 and 700,000 feet; a shape rectangular and relatively narrow with a flat ceiling and floors that did not rake too steeply; a reverberation time within the range of 1.8 seconds (Boston Symphony Hall) and 2.05 seconds (*Grosser Musikvereinsaal*).

But the answer to the sound problem wasn't quite that simple. Acoustics is part science, part guesswork. Furthermore, there was the question of which theory of sound to adopt—sound-source balance or energy-containment. The first system calls for overhead "clouds" to disperse and diffuse the sound; the second, and more traditional theory, requires a basic structure of massive stage and solid walls. The experts finally decided on the "clouds," slightly concave acoustical baffles that look like huge surfboards. Made of plaster, they are slightly more than an inch thick, about ten feet long, and a maximum of five feet wide. Lincoln Center ordered 106 of them, all to be coated with gold leaf.

Edward Downes, who writes the Philharmonic program notes, remembers talking about acoustics to the construction people. They thought it would one day be possible to change the acoustics of the hall to fit the taste and judgment of the conductor and his program—mainly by shifting the panels—but that it would be very expensive.

There were many other questions, that had to be decided. Even if they wanted to, the acoustical engineers couldn't hope to carbon-copy the concert halls in Boston and Vienna. Revised building codes and fire laws would prevent it, and so, in fact, would the changing shape of the average American. In fifty years, Americans had become bigger and broader. Just an extra inch added to both the width of the seats and the space between rows would eliminate about sixty seats. And the economics of the hall required a minimum of 2,600 seats.

A *Harvard Lampoon* poet graphically summed up the problem:

> **So theaters bought chairs to hold**
> **The bigger hip, the fatty fold,**
> **And found, to their morose chagrin,**
> **That half as many fitted in.**

The changing times also demanded more rehearsal space, a larger stage, additional electronic facilities, replacement of the plush boxes with a loge. Of course, everyone wanted air conditioning, which increased the cost of the building some twenty percent but also made possible an extended symphony season.

"As far as the style of architecture was concerned, we were perfectly aware that whatever we did was going to be wrong," said Arthur Houghton, then Chairman of the Board of the Philharmonic. "It would either be considered somewhat reactionary by the avant garde in architecture, or a little frightening because it was too advanced for the old guard. So we had to go ahead and do the best we could, and we had to do it in the style of architecture that we felt was not a whim of the moment or a monument to a particular architect. The important thing was that in the changing architectural style of the next forty years, this should still be something special and handsome. Throughout the whole project, there was an insistence on quality, quality, quality. The problem is to keep aesthetic decisions down to a handful of people, otherwise you get an adulteration of the crispness of the thing."

Max Abramovitz worked on the plans for the Hall with a team of twenty men for more than two years. Abramovitz's enthusiasm for "a glassy, open building and a day-and-night thing" never abated. He wanted to insure "a lovely place to come into, where people could meet before and after the concert and walk around during intermission. And we wanted a cafe."

Abramovitz had a lingering memory of a night in Sweden, many years before, when he had gone with friends for dinner at a theater cafe and then relaxed with coffee until the bell rang for the show. Afterwards, they returned to the cafe for drinks and conversation. "It became the whole evening, and such a pleasant one. I became enamored of the idea."

Abramovitz discarded, however, another European idea, that of separate entrances to the orchestra and to the balconies. Instead, he adopted the more democratic plan of the American movie theater, where everyone enters at the same place, and then disperses. Because of the need for space, it was also necessary for the entire audience to go one flight up to the actual hall. The interior of the hall was designed to create the aspect of a series of shallow terraces, each not more than four or five rows in depth, surrounding the main orchestra level. The idea was for the orchestra floor to "flow into the platform itself without any apparent proscenium divisions."

Most European concert halls are used experimentally for some six months before they formally open. But the Philharmonic had no time for testing. The concept of a subscription season is typically American, and the season became a controlling consideration in the planning and construction because subscription seats were sold according to the scheduled completion date.

The job of getting it done in time was given to the blunt, forceful Colonel William Powers. Powers, as assistant to Otto Nelson, had the job of supervising progress, pushing people and inspecting everything from concrete to contracts. Constant and capable help was given him by George Judd, Jr., Managing Director of the Philharmonic, and Reginald Allen, Director of Operations for Lincoln Center. Allen previously had been Manager of The Philadelphia Orchestra. "Judd and I knew exactly what the Hall had to do," he said. "The preservation of space was absolutely a must with us."

Since Philharmonic Hall was the first scheduled building in Lincoln Center, it became the construction guinea pig. Four of the largest construction companies in the country—the same companies that had built the United Nations—formed a joint venture again for this job. Each of the companies assigned a representative to work with Colonel Powers. It was hard to harmonize and supervise everything, because each firm had its own way of working and its own interpretation of the plans and prospectuses. Powers was also responsible for the complicated accounting required to assess the value of the work done by each company and for the dividing of assignments. In addition, there were as many as sixty subcontractors on this single building and constant negotiations on contracts and budgets.

To make matters even more hectic, there was the problem of integrating the work of the public garage being constructed under the buildings. The mesh of walls was such that it was difficult to decide who was to build that part of the Hall floor which was to be part of the garage ceiling, how much of it was to be paid for by the city, and

how much by Lincoln Center. Compared to all this, it was of small moment when the foundation diggers found water instead of rock in one section! An old city map revealed that it had once been a stream bed.

Water became an added problem for Powers when he was handed the headache of synchronizing the valves and programming the electronic display of the outdoor fountain. Forty pages of instructions had to be devised to produce an eight-foot-long computer tape of intricate code. This code perfected the Fountain's two sets of twenty-minute patterns going on and off with split-second timing.

One of the planned savings for the Center was a central mechanical plant to service all the buildings. A five-million-dollar investment, the system receives, meters and distributes steam to the separate buildings. And all of it was built on time, with minimum fuss and fewer than a hundred changes in final plans. But that was because not many people are interested in the aesthetics of engineering—even when the pipes are brightly colored.

George Judd died a year before the opening, and Carlos Moseley replaced him as Managing Director of the Philharmonic. Moseley had to become quickly involved in everything from carpets to organs. Two hours before the arrival of the opening-night audience, seamstresses would still be sewing the backs of rugs. As for the organ, its 5,498 pipes were so sensitive to dust that for the opening concert Moseley would have to hide six men with mops and rags behind the huge instrument to manually silence any pipes that kept on playing after they should.

To multiply the confusion, there was little time to train ushers about locations and procedures. Signs were everywhere. Elevators became temperamental. The ladies' lounge could not be finished in time so a men's room was commandeered, a new sign put on the door and drapes used to cover some of the offending plumbing.

Moseley is a gentleman of much determination. A former piano soloist with the Philharmonic, he has since become its first professional, full-time President. But at that time he needed all his reserve to cope with the chaos. Backstopping him

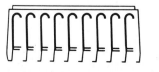

was Edgar B. Young, who was long accustomed to instant decisions. Young, Executive Vice President and previously Acting President of Lincoln Center, had long been associated with John D. Rockefeller. His presence reinforced Rockefeller's desire for perfection.

But as *Architectural Forum* magazine had warned, "If you seek to improve on the past, prepare to suffer." This was the first new concert hall built in New York City in more than a generation, and the critics were waiting.

"A friend of mine was thinking of getting involved in a smaller version of Lincoln Center, and he came to talk to me," said Arthur Houghton. "I told him, 'You're going to get criticism, whatever you do on this. Therefore, include something that everyone will focus on, and something that will not cost a great deal of money to correct.'" Houghton's friend asked him, "What would you suggest?"

"I would suggest you consider painting your lobby orange. Tell everybody in advance that you had the advice of the great color experts. People will then forget about the architecture, they'll forget about the acoustics and they'll just scream and yell about the orange color. Hold your ground for several months, then come in with a couple coats of fresh paint of another color, and you're off to the races."

"And I told him I wasn't being ironic," said Houghton. "It's just human nature, and so you have to be ready for it."

But in this instance, compliments came first.

"I find the Philharmonic Hall has its own kind of poetry," wrote *The New York Times* critic Harold C. Schonberg. "During musical performances, when the house lights are lowered, the terraces seem to melt into the midnight-blue background, and the porthole illumination vents supply a slight haze that softens the right angles where the terraces turn against the rear wall. Thanks to the comfortable seats, one's body is relaxed; and too, the broken colors of the upholstery are graceful to the eye. . . . Some critics have objected to the large glass windows. But isn't there something exciting about seeing from a distance a mass of light, broken by moving figures? A concert is, after all, a communal event. One approaches the building with an anticipatory feeling. There, seen from the outside, are the people with whom one is going to share an emotional experience. I find it thrilling and festive, and I must confess that my heart beats a little faster as I come up the block and pause to look through the glass before entering the building.

"When its central problem is overcome," added Schonberg, "Philharmonic Hall will be one of the world's great auditoriums. . . ."

The central problem, of course, was the acoustics. The "experts," amateur and professional, offered varied opinions. Some said the sound was not warm enough. Others complained that the bass response seemed to get soaked up somewhere. Some said the music did not "envelop" them, and that it was sometimes a little strident. Still others loved the sound and called it unusually clear and particularly clean in the middle registers.

Noted mezzo-soprano Jennie Tourel was utterly delighted with the new Hall. "It felt really marvelous because I didn't have the feeling of claustrophobia that you have when you sing in a small hall. A small hall just doesn't have the room to let the voice go."

Schonberg of *The Times* noted that if a soloist can produce a good sound, then it would sound good in Philharmonic Hall, but if his violin tone were thin or his piano touch percussive, then the Hall might emphasize those faults.

One official of a recording company, however, stated his open preference for the new Philharmonic Hall over Carnegie Hall. "People raised on Carnegie Hall," he commented, "couldn't take the shock of hearing all that wide-open sound."

Carnegie, of course, had had 67 years for its sound to mellow and still was never rated as top-rank. Many listeners felt it was very solid in the bass but lacked brilliance. And one violinist commented, "Listening in Carnegie is like listening with cotton in your ears."

Some acoustical faults take generations to correct. It took the Royal Albert Hall in London 98 years to get rid of a disturbing echo. Even the famous Boston Symphony Hall, so acoustically perfect, had run into severe criticism when it opened at the turn of the century. "To me, the first impression was disappointing," wrote William Foster Apthrope at that time in the

Boston *Transcript*. "The tone . . . had no life, there was nothing commanding and compelling about it."

What made matters more critical was that the new Philharmonic Hall had had no shakedown period in which to test and correct. Foam-rubber-filled dummies had been brought in as a simulated audience, but no provision had been made for the reverberation from starched tuxedo shirts of a first-night audience. The experts, however, had provided the Hall with a safety factor by leaving a sizable air space between roof and ceiling so that the ceiling could be opened, raised or removed.

So much was written about the Hall's acoustics that some curious people even asked the ushers, "Where are the acoustics?" Carlos Moseley received letters from amateur experts who knew exactly how to correct the problems, and one of them wired, "I told your associates that I am the only man who can correct the acoustics of your Hall without all the hulaballoo."

Max Abramovitz was more realistic about the situation. "This thing is like jelly; you put your finger in here, and something else goes out."

The several attempts at patchwork solutions brought small results. Amyas Ames, then President of the Philharmonic and now Chairman of the Board, made the basic decision for a complete overhaul.

"I'm a great admirer of George Szell, and he told me what a great job Heinrich Keilholz had done for the acoustics of the Severance Hall in Cleveland," Ames remembered. "So we got Keilholz. He's a marvelous man with a sensitive ear for music, and he talks the language of musicians. Keilholz puts more emphasis on the human ear than on all these electronic measuring devices. And he believes in the classic use of wood that has worked acoustical wonders for centuries. He also believes in a minimum of upholstery and carpeting. What he said was that the old-fashioned ballroom with its hard, wood floor, its curved wooden boxes and balconies, its gilt chairs and crystal chandeliers, has always been one of the finest places in which to hear music."

Keilholz proposed that they change the smooth walls by superimposing curved wooden reflecting surfaces. Then he suggested unstuffing the over-stuffed chairs (which then provided enough extra

space for 178 more seats). And, finally, Keilholz recommended replacing the "clouds" with a solid wooden ceiling. Instead of deflecting the sound, the clouds had muffled it. A solid ceiling, he said, would bounce the sound to the listening ear more quickly.

In addition to the acoustical changes, Ames decided to redecorate the Hall. Abe Feder designed lights diffused through crystal to give a soft, shimmering effect; Felicia Bernstein and Donald Oenslager devised a decor keyed to the natural color of acacia wood walls: offwhite for the ceiling, a light red fabric for the seats to give a greater sense of intimacy. With this new reflected lightness, the artist for the first time could see the audience.

The total cost for the renovation was estimated at $1.3 million, and the big question was: Where would this money come from?

Lincoln Center, Inc., deep in its own budget crisis, couldn't help. Ames made the gamble to go it alone. Mrs. John D. Rockefeller, Jr., pledged an initial $250,000; some $400,000 came from the future income of the new seats. Somehow, all the money was soon raised.

Down came the clouds; up went heavy ply-wood panels, averaging twelve feet long by six feet wide (it took six men to lift one of them). The job was completed in the summer of 1969. The musical minds had replaced the electronic experts.

The new acoustics were a complete success. *The New York Times* headline read:

NEW PHILHARMONIC SOUND GLOWS

Nobody was more pleased than Philharmonic Hall Manager Patrick McGinnis. When the earlier critics were less than kind, it was McGinnis who pointed out the Hall's marvelous isolation from external sound. "You don't hear the subway, you don't hear the jet noises, you don't hear outside fire trucks." McGinnis also stressed that the stage could be seen from any seat in the Hall, whereas at Carnegie Hall, there are some 300 seats listed as "partial views."

Patrick McGinnis is the "worry man" for the Hall. He worries about the durability of curtains in the sunlight; the tricky job of dusting the sculpture—Richard Lippold's five-ton, 190-foot long stabile suspended from the ceiling; the budget for light bulbs—$6,500 a year; the two men who

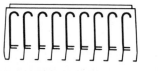

continually wash glass every day, every week, all year round; the terrazzo floors that have to be regularly stripped, resealed and re-buffed; the mohair wearing out on the armrests of the seats. To help him worry, McGinnis has a staff of more than a hundred people.

"I'm the landlord here," McGinnis says, "my job is to keep the tenants happy."

The principal tenant, of course, is the New York Philharmonic. The Philharmonic plays about 150 performances a year at the Hall including 33 weeks of subscription series and another four weeks of summer Promenades. (It also has four weeks of concerts in the parks, plus tours.) This averages three evening performances and one matinee each week. But the Philharmonic also holds all its rehearsals in the Hall, as well as most of its recording sessions.

Philharmonic Hall, however, still has time and space for some five hundred other events in the course of an average year. These include everything from a Sunday service of the Church of the Truth to a college commencement to an international choral festival to a rock or jazz concert to a Happening with Salvador Dali. More regular events are the concerts of visiting symphony orchestras—Boston, Philadelphia, Washington National, among others.

Stage logistics can become enormously intricate. "It's amazing how quickly you can build up to three hundred people backstage," said McGinnis. "Roughly a hundred in the orchestra, and then some of the large choral works call for a male chorus, a female chorus and a children's chorus. That's a lot of people with a lot of wardrobe trunks and a lot of instrument trunks."

But they've got that all down to a system now —just as they've developed a technique for handling busloads of children for the student matinees by using color-coded maps designating group and seating area.

The most complicated logistics in the Hall, however, is the massive three-day changeover from the regular concert season to the Promenades summer concerts. This job means some twenty-five stagehands in three eight-hour shifts. The seats are replaced with platforms to level the floor, then tables and chairs are added—and suddenly, the whole tone of the Hall changes.

"I don't know a single place anywhere else in the world where this happens," said André Kostelanetz, who organizes, directs and conducts the Promenades concerts with the Philharmonic. "Music must not bore, and I'm afraid we would get bored doing the same kind of Promenades over and over again. So every year we try to create something new, not just musically, but visually. Every year the audience walks in here and says, 'I've never seen this. Where are we?' That's what we want: different colors, different design, different set-up on the stage, different program. It's the idea of the eye being important to the ear."

A young designer named Peter Wexler has helped to develop the main theme for each summer's Promenades. One year the entire Hall took on the appearance of the prow of a giant ship. "I was there at eight in the morning with the workmen, and my heart was in my mouth," said Kenneth Haas, Assistant to the Manager of the Philharmonic and Coordinator of the Promenades. "I really expected the whole thing to fall down because the man who made the ribbons had weighted them with 300 pounds of lead so they wouldn't blow away. I kept thinking, all this crepe paper, tissue paper, loaded down with all that lead! And, sure enough, the whole thing started to sag. So I called the rigger and he rigged up some more clamps, hooked them on each of the poles in the middle, and held it together with more C-clamps from the top of the building, with a million guy-wires all over it. And it worked. It really did look like the prow of a ship. It was just lovely."

The summer Promenades have brought in a whole new audience, many of whom had never been to Philharmonic Hall before. Basically, it's a younger audience. They find a gay atmosphere of flowers and color and paintings and exhibits. Many of them come early, look at everything leisurely and dine amid all the excitement.

Dining, however, is strictly secondary. When the bells ring to announce the beginning of the concert, every waiter in the Grand Promenade area must leave. "We always have to remember that we're running a concert hall, not the Waldorf," said Moseley.

Always interested in a fresh, new approach, Kostelanetz keeps a large envelope into which he stuffs ideas for the coming year's Promenades. He successfully keeps his programs a mixture of the experimental and the unexpected: a modern dance, a newly commissioned work; the score of *Lady Macbeth*; a ballet for a Verdi opera that hasn't been played for forty years; William Schuman's *New England Triptych*; "The Story of Babar the Elephant"; even some newly discovered light music written by Shostakovich for comic plays and motion pictures.

"The Russians never recorded that for some reason," said Kostelanetz, speaking of the newly found Shostakovich pieces, "but Carlos Moseley found a tape of it that the Germans had used. Things like that give zest to our Promenades. Zest is a good word for the tone of what we try to do."

"It's funny how the use of the Hall evolved," reminisced Roger Englander, who produced some of the early Promenades seasons and who has produced and directed all the Young People's Concerts for the Philharmonic. "At first the Hall was a very pristine place and nothing extraneous could get into it. But in the course of years, it has become more of a living thing—greenery, sculpture, traveling exhibits."

While much has changed with the Philharmonic Orchestra in the new Hall, there are many basic things that have remained the same. Frank Milburn still has the headache of scheduling the soloists to avoid repetition and of arranging dates to avoid overlapping. Moreover he must carefully check the programs of all visiting orchestras: "You can't have Beethoven on every program." Milburn does his program planning two years in advance.

Actual contract negotiations, however, are the concern of Assistant Manager William Weissel. Assistant managers are involved with everything "from the sublime to the ridiculous," said Weissel, "and one might negotiate a million-dollar contract

in the morning, then make sure that the conductor has his favorite towel waiting for him in his dressing room in the evening."

Subscription series tickets are also handled long in advance. "We can fill the house over and over again," said Mrs. Helen Franklin, head of the subscription department. But at least one hundred seats are withheld from subscription sale and are put out for box-office sale four weeks in advance of each concert. More than an equivalent number of seats are put aside for certain concerts to accommodate students at a special reduced rate.

Whether the Philharmonic travels to Russia or to Central Park, the musicians still take tons of instruments and equipment. Production Manager Hal DeWindt is in charge of the complicated logistics and stage representative Frank Nelson is in charge of making sure that the 100 trunks are all assembled. "Sometimes I wonder how the airplane gets off the ground," Nelson said. At the Hall itself, the musicians have plenty of storage space.

Some modern compositions require electric organs, electric pianos, electric guitars and even more esoteric instruments such as the Onde Martinot. The Martinot is a kind of piano with a ribbon that is pulled to magnify the sound (in all of New York, there's only one musician, a woman, who plays that instrument). Odd instruments and special effects are usually rented, but there are exceptions. One modern composition called for the sound of bottles breaking, and the Philharmonic simply sent out to a nearby cafe for several dozen ordinary bottles, put them in a pail and covered it with canvas to protect the bottle-breaker from flying glass. "But it was really a mess," said Joseph de Angelis, who had played solo bass in the Philharmonic and later was Personnel Manager.

There isn't much turnover among musicians at the New York Philharmonic, because most musicians consider this level as the apex of achievement. But the 106 members may be increased to 125 for certain compositions, and the Personnel Manager has to know where to find the extra players, and to be prepared to get instant substitutes for any musicians who are sick or

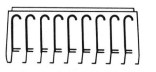

otherwise unavailable. In addition to all this he serves as a liaison between the complaints of the musicians and the needs of the conductor.

"You just can't please everybody," de Angelis remarked. "For example, some musicians love the air conditioning, and some don't. It depends sometimes where they sit. And some musicians work up a sweat faster than others."

Engelbert Brenner, an English-horn player approaching his fortieth year with the Philharmonic, explained that complaint more personally: "It's like when five fellows get into a poker game. All of a sudden, the coldest room will seem warm. It's difficult with more than a hundred of us—some of us are emotionally more upset than others when we have to play a solo. The string players like it a little more cool, and the wind players a little more warm. Cooler temperature gives the strings a more brittle and cutting sound, which they particularly prefer when recording. But when you play a metal instrument, like a flute, or a woodwind instrument—the condensation can cause them to act like distilleries. You blow warm air in and it can create bubbles.

"I worry about gurgles," Brenner continued. "When we play the *Symphony Fantastique*, I sit there for three movements, then begin cold, alone. And I really go through agony hoping that the first note will not be a gurgle. It can happen." Nonetheless Brenner remembers that "it was murder to play in Carnegie Hall on a hot day," and he added how marvelous it was that the air conditioning had extended the symphony season.

"We used to work only 25 weeks a year at most, so there were 27 weeks during which you had little or nothing to do. It was very difficult for families to make ends meet."

Engelbert Brenner, therefore, is willing to tolerate the threat of the gurgles.

Musicians also complained occasionally about the acoustics. Again, it depended upon where they sat. There were dead spots on stage where the musicians couldn't hear each other play. "But I played at Carnegie Hall for thirty years," Brenner said, "and I can tell you that there were dead spots on that stage, too." "Now we can hear each other," said David Nadien, the concertmaster, after the most recent acoustical corrections. "We can pay attention to the differences between forte and mezzoforte," added Walter Rosenberger, the percussionist.

What delights all the musicians in Philharmonic Hall is the sheer comfort and cleanliness of it, and the space. "They're even making a special ladies' room for the girl cellist and myself," said lovely young Orin O'Brien, who plays the bass, and is the only other woman in the orchestra. "I've even heard rumors that they're fixing up a special little place for us with a hot plate, so we can make tea or something."

The high regard of the Philharmonic for women was recently demonstrated again when Mrs. Helen Thompson became the new Managing Director. Mrs. Thompson helped organize the American Symphony Orchestra League in 1943 and is the first woman ever to manage a major American orchestra. She herself was a violinist.

There are thirty-four violinists in the New York Philharmonic and eighteen of them from the First Violin section. One is Kenneth Gordon, who made his debut at the age of twelve as a soloist with the NBC Symphony Orchestra under Leopold Stokowski, studied with Koussevitzky at Tanglewood, and played concerts in every major city in the world. He joined the New York Philharmonic in 1961.

Gordon detailed the typical work week of a Philharmonic musician during the season: Rehearsal Monday morning, concert that night. A free day on Tuesday unless recording sessions are scheduled. Wednesday calls for two rehearsals, morning and afternoon. Thursday, another rehearsal for the concert that night. Two more concerts on Friday and Saturday. If something new and complicated is scheduled, there may also be rehearsals on Tuesday morning.

It becomes even more complicated when there are visiting conductors, each with his own style. Gordon explained the importance of the conductor:

"Don't forget that when you're ready to play, you have more than a hundred individuals who have come from different walks of life. Maybe one musician had a fight with his wife that morning, or his kids annoyed him or he didn't sleep well or he has a big bill to pay. All these guys come that particular evening at 8:30, with all of their own worries, to play a program of beautiful music, which people have paid good money to hear. How do you get all these guys to play as one? And to think as one voice? It has to be the conductor. I think the conductor has to be not only a great technician with his baton, but a great psychologist. He has to know how to instill a great amount of excitement in his men to get them to play the very best they can."

Critics have referred to the meticulousness of Koussevitzky with the Boston Symphony, the sensuous sound of The Philadelphia Symphony with Stokowski, and the intensity of Toscanini with the NBC Symphony.

"Toscanini was not excessively emotional and demonstrative," Engelbert Brenner added, "but his hands would sort of clench, and you could feel it—it was coming from *inside*. Mitropolous was very emotional. He brought excitement. It wasn't all clear music, but he excited people. Now Lenny seems to have a little bit of all of them. But there's a greater feeling of intimacy with him." ("Lenny," of course, is Leonard Bernstein, whom Brenner as well as many of the other Philharmonic musicians have known for almost thirty years. On stage, though, they are more likely to call him, "Maestro.")

Brenner teaches at Juilliard, and he explains the distinctions among conductors by telling his students, "Look, you can tell someone, 'I love you.' You can also say, 'I LOVE YOU!' And you can whisper, 'I *love* you.' There are great differences."

The Philharmonic has many visiting conductors, and the musicians say this is very tricky because each conductor has his own method of beating time. Some are as precise as the second hand of a watch. Others use great sweeping motions, a manner which permits the player far more freedom. Some emphasize large phrasing, so that if they don't see the precise beat, it doesn't matter because the sound is there—tremendous sound.

"It's better for a young conductor to conduct the Philharmonic than to make his debut with a smaller orchestra," said Kenneth Gordon, "because he's always going to get a first-rate performance from the Philharmonic. A young conductor can goof, but the orchestra plays on. It's a story some musicians tell: If they ever

looked up and saw the beat from a young, new conductor, they'd fall apart."

This is particularly true of the older, more standard symphonies, which the musicians know almost instinctively now. "I like modern music," said Brenner, "because you've got to think about it."

One man who thinks about all the music is the librarian Howard Keresey, who shared the responsibility with Joseph Zizza until the latter's recent death. Several thousand packages fill the shelves of the large, airy room, each package usually containing the orchestration of one work. These are the standard works included in the repertoire of almost every leading symphonic orchestra. Keresey and Zizza were not only the keepers of the copies, but they had to make all the requested changes and corrections for all instruments of any given piece of music.

The bulk of the editing is on standard repertoire. "In many instances," Zizza had pointed out, "Bach didn't even bother to put down whether the music was to be played softly or loudly, much less anything as daring as a retard or an acceleration. He just wrote notes."

"In Stravinsky's *Sacre du Printemps*," Keresey explained, "there was a list of errata with some 300 discrepancies—sharps that should have been flats, omissions, wrong clefs. But in some cases, we don't know where the mistakes are until the thing is actually in rehearsal. Studying the piece, the conductor will *hear* a wrong note and then indicate to us what should be corrected."

Some conductors might also want a *mezzo piano* instead of the *piano* indicated in the score. Others might want to change the dynamics in a certain place. Both Keresey and Zizza admired the way Leonard Bernstein can regroup the bars of very complicated rhythm to make it easier to play, while still not destroying the accents intended by the composer. And a librarian always has to be on the lookout for "bad turns" at the bottom of a page of music. "In one edition of the Brahms B-Flat Concerto," Zizza said, "there's a bad turn in the middle of a cello solo. Now how can the guy possibly play the cello and turn the page?"

Composer Aaron Copland joins in the admiration of Bernstein. "Bernstein knows audience reaction to new pieces even before he

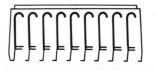

plays them," he said. "People can adjust to new plays or new ballets more quickly than they can to new music. The difference, perhaps, is between the visual and the aural. I don't know why. But many composers shy away from writing new symphonies—so few orchestras will play them because of this conservative audience reaction."

But not Bernstein. Most critics have credited him with a flair for modern music—a forward drive—so that the strangest complex of sound still comes out, somehow, in a flow. In the terminology of music critics, his conducting has shape as well as color, structural integrity as well as freedom within the phrase. These words have more meaning when you see Bernstein at a rehearsal. Focusing on a tuba player to pull out a certain quality, he called, "Fortissimo," then pleaded, "Aw, come on," and finally, "That's more like it, that's very good." At another point, he turned to the young composer seated in the audience and asked, "Is that the way you want it?"

"A bigger crescendo," the composer answered.

During his time with the Philharmonic, Bernstein put great emphasis on the search for new composers.

"I think symphonic music, the world over, has reached an historic curve, an arch, that began with Mozart and ended with Mahler," he said. "What kept it growing all those beautiful years between Mozart and Mahler were the composers themselves who kept demanding more virtuosity, more sensitivity of performance. But then the orchestra itself attained its final shape, which hasn't changed since then and shows no signs of changing. That doesn't mean the symphonic orchestra is over, by any means. It can go on forever being a great and glorious kind of museum, playing these repertoire works. And I'm still hoping, of course, that there are still other avenues of growth. But if we want some kind of freshness, there's got to be money for it. We've got to commission more and more new works because the modern composer no longer thinks in terms of symphony orchestra."

David Amram does. In 1967 Amram was the New York Philharmonic's first Composer in Residence at Lincoln Center. Before that, he had written eighty-three works and had also served as

Music Director for the Repertory Theater in Lincoln Center. Amram offered his views of the development of symphonic music:

"There are a lot of snobbish people who really want to keep Art as a kind of an inside private thing, and who feel that if a lot of people enjoy symphonic music or opera, then it can't be any good anymore. But I think that symphonic music is just beginning. The form of symphonic music is changing, just as it always has. I'm sure that when Beethoven enlarged the orchestra, a lot of people must have thought that symphonic music was finished. Yet they still play Mozart and Haydn symphonies today, and they're just as delightful to listen to. The orchestra was expanded up to the time of Mahler and Richard Strauss to about as large as it could get. Then it started getting smaller again. Now a lot of composers are writing for very small groups, but that's partly because they know they can get their music performed that way. But I have at least two dozen letters from conductors who want to play my music and I'm writing a full symphony now, and I plan to write much more, because I now know that someone will play them.

"There's an enormous audience who want to hear symphony orchestras play. If we can only inspire enough composers who come from divergent backgrounds with experience in American music like folk and jazz—and who are interested in music as a totality and not trying so hard to hang onto the heels of the latest innovations—then there's going to be a terrific renaissance and rebirth of writing for the symphony orchestra. In Poland, there are lots of people writing for the symphony, and they're doing some fantastic music. A lot of South American composers have written great orchestra music. And I'm looking forward to hearing more symphonic music that Mr. Bernstein writes when he has more time."

After ten active years as Music Director of the Philharmonic, Leonard Bernstein has retired to the lifetime title of "Laureate Conductor." This will give him more time to compose music—of all kinds.

Pierre Boulez, the new Music Director, will now concentrate on the long-range future of the Philharmonic.

Pierre Boulez represents a considerable contrast to Bernstein. If Bernstein is more interested in the mood and emotion of music, Boulez is more concerned with its organization and structure. Boulez is regarded as the spokesman of the avant garde, specializing in the 12-tone music that stems from Schoenberg and has dominated the international music of the twentieth century.

Boulez's personal preferences, however, do not distort his performance. Composer Darius Milhaud once said of him, "He despises my music but conducts it better than anyone."

Still in his early forties Boulez will be the first Frenchman to head America's oldest symphony orchestra. At the same time, he will also act as head of London's BBC Symphony Orchestra and retain several months a year for his own composing. Boulez has been called the single most important force in contemporary music. And the orchestra's President, Carlos Moseley said, "We look forward to some innovations from Mr. Boulez. We expect offbeat concerts and excitement and packed houses. He's a real pied piper."

Boulez works without a baton or a score, and with a minimum of dramatics. He has described the baton as "a one-handed hook which keeps you from expressing with your fingers."

"He's not a 'show-biz' conductor," said violinist Jack Fishberg, "but he can hear a pin drop and tell you what key it's in." And David Nadien, the Philharmonic concertmaster added, "Boulez has one of the clearest stick techniques I've ever seen. We need a good traffic cop up there and he's a good one, musically."

Music traffic cop or pied piper, Pierre Boulez has his own ideas about the Philharmonic:

"Let's not have a museum, let's have a laboratory," he said. "Why be afraid of flouting tradition?'

Some fifty years ago the Chicago Symphony Orchestra performed Brahms in this country for the first time, and the audience didn't like it. Conductor Frederick Stock said, "Well, I will repeat this work until you do like this experience." And so he did, until they did.

The future of the New York Philharmonic is not the future of a museum; it is the future of a searching, sensitive musical instrument always attempting to be in tune with its time.

The legendary Arturo Toscanini.

(1) Carnegie Hall, for many years the home of the New York Philharmonic.

(2) Carl Sandburg recites *A Lincoln Portrait* by Aaron Copland, with André Kostelanetz conducting the Philharmonic, at a rehearsal for the Carnegie Hall performance in February, 1956.

(3) Poster by the noted artist Ben Shahn for the opening of Philharmonic Hall.

(4) In the rush to get the Hall ready for opening night, seamstresses work on the carpeting as the orchestra rehearses on stage.

(5) The skeletal framework of Philharmonic Hall just a few months earlier.

LINCOLN CENTER
FOR THE PERFORMING ARTS

PHILHARMONIC HALL
OPENING SEPTEMBER 23,19

3

5   BOB SERATING

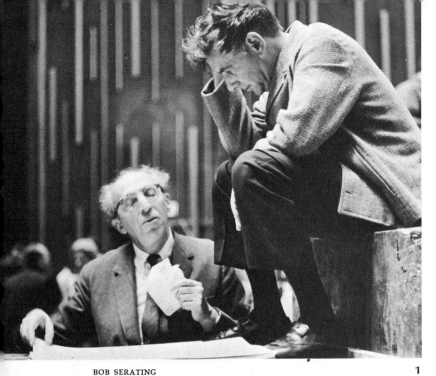

BOB SERATING   **1**

BOB SERATING   **2**

BOB SERATING   **3**   **4**   GUY GILLETTE

Opening Night of Philharmonic Hall,
September 23, 1962

(1) During "Tuning Week" prior to the opening of the Hall, composer Aaron Copland (*left*) works with Leonard Bernstein, Music Director of the New York Philharmonic.

(2) Just before the pre-opening concert, William Schuman, now President Emeritus of Lincoln Center, greets Concertmaster John Corigliano. Carlos Moseley, Managing Director of the New York Philharmonic, is at left.

(3) Among the many distinguished guests were U Thant, Secretary General of the United Nations, and Adlai E. Stevenson, U.S. Representative to the United Nations. To their left are Mr. and Mrs. Samuel J. Bernstein, the parents of Leonard Bernstein.

(4) The First Lady, representing President John F. Kennedy, and John D. Rockefeller 3rd.

Leonard Bernstein conducting the New York Philharmonic orchestra.

1

2
3

Some of the guest conductors of the New York Philharmonic:
(1) the incomparable Danny Kaye;
(2) young Seiji Ozawa, who was also an assistant conductor with the Philharmonic;
(3) Pierre Boulez, the New York Philharmonic's new Music Director.

(4) Some members of the New York Philharmonic.

(5) Intermission at Philharmonic Hall.

4

5

CBS PHOTO 1
BOB SERATING 2

LEE JOHNSON FOR SHELL NEWS

BOB SERATING

3
4

(1) A Young People's Concert, conducted by Alois Springer, Dimitri Mitropoulos prize winner, with Lawrence Foster as cello soloist.

(2) A painting on the theme of "What Lincoln Center Means to Me" by Richard Alvarez, fifth grade, for the Student Art Exhibit.

(3) An absorbed audience at a Young People's Concert.

(4) Bronze "Tragic Mask of Beethoven" by Antoine Bourdelle in Philharmonic Hall.

E. FRED SHER   **1**

ALFRED STATLER, FOR THE NEW YORK PHILHARMONIC   **2**

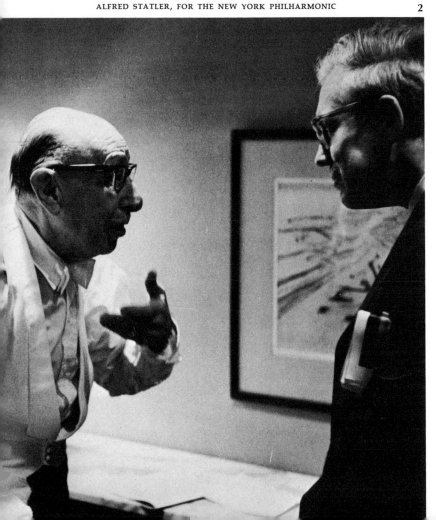

(1) Pierre Boulez (*center*) new Music Director of the New York Philharmonic with Carlos Moseley (*left*), President of the Philharmonic Symphony-Society of New York, and Amyas Ames, Chairman of the Board of the Symphony-Society and of Lincoln Center.

(2) Composers Igor Stravinsky (*left*) and Elliott Carter at Philharmonic Hall's "Stravinsky Festival."

(3) Philharmonic Hall.

the
new york
state
theater

"I designed it for George."
—Architect Philip Johnson referring to
the State Theater

George, of course, is George Balanchine, one of the world's great choreographers and Director of the New York City Ballet. And Philip Johnson, of course, is one of the world's great architects. Balanchine and Johnson and Lincoln Kirstein—who brought Balanchine to the United States—had begun discussing their ideal dance theater back in the 1930's. They talked of it often, in great detail, and lovingly. During the evolution of the Lincoln Center concept—when the New York City Ballet was invited to be a constituent—Balanchine and Kirstein, along with Governor Nelson Rockefeller, wanted Philip Johnson to be the architect of their dance theater.

The first design called for a semicircular front and all the interior details they had originally planned. "Then it was compromise, compromise, compromise," emphasized Balanchine.

One reason for the compromise was the fact that the State Theater was not only to be a home for dance, but also for the New York City Opera and, later, the Music Theater. Naturally each company had different needs.

Balanchine's primary concern was the stage. The stage at the State Theater is bigger than the one they had at City Center, and the ballets look better on it. The adjustment of pipes for hanging scenery took time, "but now it works," Balanchine said. The side stages could be bigger "but they will do." The orchestra members now have a lounge, "but the pit is too small to create a proper sound from sixty musicians."

The budget called for many other compromises. Originally there were supposed to be four ballet studios, each the size of the stage, for full rehearsals. These were cut to one large and three small ones. "But the thing is that we have three resident companies sharing the space of this single building," said General Manager Betty Cage. "The three of us have a very friendly relationship. We accommodate each other when we can and we have tried to cope with almost any limitations."

Despite the technical limitations, the New York State Theater is a building of much beauty. Its exterior is sober and rational, and this feeling of solidity creates a striking contrast to its glass-walled sister building across the plaza, Philharmonic Hall. Both structures are nine stories high, faced in travertine and fronted with columns, and there their similarity of style ends.

For all the sobriety of the exterior, the interior of the State Theater is festive and elegant.

The tone is set by the great public area on the floor above the lobby. It is a royal room of cream and gold, almost two hundred feet long and half again as high and wide. Ringing it are three serried balconies, railed with gilt grills that are delicately filigreed. The effect is dramatic and stunning. Overlooking everything at both ends of the room are enormous twin marble ladies, each carved out of a single block of stone. A critic described them as "direct descendents of Caryatids on circus calliopes, clipper ship figure-heads and cigar store Indians, even with a hint of burlesque queens . . . the baroque spirit domesticated by democracy." Governor Nelson Rockefeller has a bronze casting of one of the originals in his garden at Pocantico Hills. They are the work of the Polish-American sculptor, Elie Nadelman.

The auditorium inside is horseshoe-shaped, with five tiers of shallow balconies above the orchestra level. With this horseshoe design, no orchestra seat is more than 140 feet from the stage. And the shallow balconies are so carefully recessed one above the other, that sight lines are generally excellent. The balconies sweep around the sides of the hall to the proscenium arch so that the walls seem animated with people. Orchestra seating is continental, with no center aisles, and that adds to the sense of intimacy. Lincoln Kirstein described this auditorium as being "a quiet dialogue between amplitude and intimacy."

It has been said of Lincoln Edward Kirstein that no other American has done more for the art of ballet. It was Kirstein who persuaded George Balanchine to start a school of American ballet. The two men initiated their dance company in 1933 and though suffering a series of financial failures, they began a new direction in dance. Out of their venture grew such well-known American

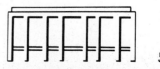

55

ballets as *Billy the Kid* by Eugene Loring with a score by Aaron Copland, and Lew Christensen's *Filling Station*, its score by Virgil Thomson. Their American Ballet Caravan later toured Latin America under the sponsorship of a State Department cultural program headed by Nelson Rockefeller.

Then Kirstein and Balanchine formed Ballet Society, aimed at presenting only new ballets. The group rented New York City Center for four performances, and in the audience was Morton Baum, Chairman of City Center's Executive Committee.

Baum was so impressed by the ballets he saw that he offered the company a permanent home at City Center. Kirstein told him then, "In three years, I promise you the greatest company in the world." The promise was kept.

By 1952 the New York City Ballet had triumphed all over Europe. It was the first foreign company to dance at the Paris Opera House and La Scala in Milan, and it became the highlight of a dozen international festivals. Then the Ford Foundation gave a ten-year grant of $4 million to the company's School of American Ballet, and American ballet moved out of a shaky adolescence into maturity.

Kirstein was an early member of the exploratory group that developed the Lincoln Center concept, but he quit after an unresolved serious difference of opinion. A description of Lincoln Kirstein in the Literary Supplement of the London *Times* remarked:

"Lincoln Kirstein, Balanchine's lieutenant, is ubiquitous and so unreliable . . . that an exact estimation of his position is difficult. Well-off, erratic, with a public manner so prickly that his chief talent seems to be for making enemies and alienating people, it might seem that, after so long a time, he could afford to relax."

In accordance with the *Times*' custom, the article was unsigned. But a number of highly informed people felt free to assert that it was written by—Lincoln Kirstein.

Kirstein's departure from Lincoln Center's Executive Board did not interfere with their mutual determination to create a new home for American dance. The New York State Theater was the second building to be completed in the Center; its opening date was April 23, 1964.

The New York City Ballet gave immediate stature to the State Theater. Philip Johnson had set out to design the Theater for George Balanchine because the New York City Ballet *is* Balanchine. But Balanchine says of himself, "I don't create. God creates."

"I assemble, and I steal from everywhere to do it—from what I see, from what the dancers can do, from what others do. . . . Without dancers I can do nothing. Some choreographers work out all their ballets by dancing themselves in front of a mirror. Then they write it all down. I don't do that. To me, ballet exists only when people are performing. When I use dancers, I want to make things for their bodies to do. . . . Steps don't exist in themselves. I try to find interesting proportions of movement in time and space. I don't think lots; I just manipulate. I never think in advance of what movement I need; I have to have a person, not an idea. Many choreographers would not agree with me, but my idea is that what is important about dancing is the dancers, because the dancer *is* the choreography. Choreography doesn't exist on paper or in somebody's mind; it exists only in living bodies and motion.

"Sometimes, people say to me, 'Wouldn't it be wonderful if you could use a system of notation so you could just sit at home and write choreography without having to come to your ballet studio?' I can't imagine ever doing it. I wouldn't be interested, absolutely not! If I didn't have dancers in front of me, I would never choreograph."

In his excellent biography *Balanchine*, Bernard Taper gave this description of George Balanchine at work:

"The first thing he may do is arrange the dancers, in various poses, here and there about the room, in the pictorial composition they will form when the curtain rises.

"As they hold their places, he stands before them in silence, his hands clasped, head slightly bowed; he is listening to the first phrase of the music within him and summoning up in his mind's eye the dance phrase he will match to it— a phrase that consists of five or six different movements by different soloists or groups at the same time. Standing there, he suggests a chess master planning a move. From the room next door, where other members of the company are rehearsing some other work, comes the sound of a piano thumping away, but it does not seem to penetrate Balanchine's concentration. As the dance ideas occur to him, his hands unclasp and his fingers come to life, as if they were dancing in the air. 'All right,' Balanchine says, stepping over to one of his soloists—the principal ballerina, perhaps—'you do like this.' And he dances out for her the steps he has conceived, counting aloud each beat of the phrase as he does so. She immediately reproduces his movements while echoing his count. 'And you,' Balanchine says, turning next, perhaps to the leading male dancer, you do like *this*.'

"In the same way, he produces sequences for the other soloists and the ensembles of the corps de ballet. When he has communicated in his way all the movements of the dance phrase, he will have the pianist play the few bars of music for it while the dancers put it together for his scrutiny. He may have them run through it several times more, and he may tinker with it or even discard it and try a fresh approach, but often it will be just the way he wants it from the start. With a brief nod, he murmurs, 'Tha-ats right.' The dancers store their steps away in their remarkable muscle memories, and Balanchine, in the same manner as before, takes up the next phrase."

Choreographer Agnes de Mille described a Balanchine "assembling" on the stage by saying, "It's like watching light pass through a prism. The music passes through him, and in the same natural yet marvelous way that a prism refracts light, he refracts music into dance."

"He seems as soft as silk, but he's as tough as steel," said Kirstein of Balanchine. "He's the most secure man I ever met in my life. He has authority to the nth degree."

Balanchine seldom works with the full cast for more than a few hours at a time, so his new ballets come alive piece by piece, section by section, almost like the making of a movie. Variety refreshes him, he claims, so he often works on several ballets at a time, sometimes switching from a sad one to a brassy one to something avant garde. His dancers wait for him patiently.

"That's the way we have to do it," Balanchine added. "They wait and I think. That's their business, and we each do our job.

"These people who say, 'The dancing was great, but the music and choreography were lousy,'—I do not understand them. Not when the dance grows right out of the music."

"What we call ballet," said Lincoln Kirstein, "is a mixture in space of human anatomy, solid geometry and musical measurement." And then he added, "Dance is the poetry of space come alive in the measure of time."

Balanchine has repeatedly said that a person planning to attend the ballet for the first time "should come and see, come and discover. . . . Then if he comes again and again and stares—sure enough, the fifth or sixth time, he will see how beautiful it is, how the air becomes transparent, and you can smell it; there is a glow—the space, the hands, everything is fantastically beautiful. And he wants to see more."

Balanchine considers ballet predominantly female—women can do without men in a ballet, but men cannot have a ballet company without women. "Male dancers don't like to hear it, but I believe it," he insists. "They are very important as princes and attendants to the queen, but Woman is the queen."

One of the recent queens of the New York City Ballet was lovely young Suzanne Farrell. "It's important to recognize a dancer," said Balanchine, "like a jewel. You faint from its beauty. I don't only like young dancers. But it's my business to start them young. If I didn't, there wouldn't be any old dancers."

Balanchine auditioned Suzanne Farrell when she was fifteen. She had studied at the Conservatory of Music in Cincinnati, where she was seen by dancer Diana Adams who recommended her to Balanchine's School of American Ballet in Manhattan. The Ford Foundation gave her a scholarship, and she and her mother and sister moved to New York.

In her diary, the 15-year-old Suzanne wrote:
"Mr. Balanchine watched class for about five minutes today. I felt like a klutz. Jacques

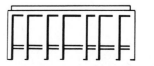

57

d'Amboise was my partner in adagio class! Wow! He's so cute. You get the message. We watched the New York City Ballet rehearsing—through a crack in the door. I went to Capezio's to buy some toe shoes. I bought the 'Nicolini' but I'm switching to the 'Assoluta.' You'll never guess what happened. I was chosen for an angel in *The Nutcracker.* And Mr. Balanchine asked me my name. Wish me luck! I have far-fetched dreams. We ate at the Automat as usual."

At the age of nineteen Suzanne Farrell became one of the youngest principal dancers in the history of the New York City Ballet.

"You wonder, 'Will I make it?' It's tough," she said. "Dancing can be physically trying and depressing for your morale. . . . We all work so hard—people, even my mother, see only the beauty, not the kids coming offstage and collapsing. . . . And there's always the anxiety of whether you're doing the right thing. . . . Mr. Balanchine says it's all right to make mistakes, it's only bad when you don't know why you made them."

Those who know claim that the discipline of a dancer is more intense than that of a boxer in training for a championship fight, and the grace of a great dancer is as rare as that of a great bullfighter. Like them, a dancer never stops training throughout his career.

"If you have any brains," added soloist Carol Sumner, "you come early and warm up, or break an ankle." Some dancers complain that Balanchine's training exercises are too demanding, too merciless. But one dancer said, "When Mr. B. first demanded sixteen *tendus,* I thought he was off his rocker. Now I feel gypped if he doesn't. The more you do, the more you see you can do, and the harder you try."

"A dancer is a musical instrument," said Balanchine. "It must be played with a full-bodied tone—and pitilessly."

Balanchine, who was ballet master for the famous Diaghilev Company in Monto Carlo before coming to New York, has firm views on the differences between dancers then and now: "Today's dancers are better in almost every way," he said. "They are much more disciplined, more serious, more musical, faster, have better

technique—and they are better-looking, too. A girl from the New York City corps de ballet today would probably be as capable as a ranking ballerina in the Maryinsky Company. As for the famous Diaghilev Company, it was absolutely awful in the quality of its dancing. It was full of awkward, poorly trained, rather ugly people. . . . The old dancers were short, with big busts and behinds, and corsets, and all that hair piled up with bird-of-paradise feathers in it. Now we have stripped the girls almost naked; who wants to see a costume dance? We have taller, better-looking dancers, and they are a million times better."

Compared to Europeans, the new American breed of ballet dancers is regarded as faster, sharper, slimmer and more energetic. One critic, calling the New York City Ballet, "the best-looking company in the world," declared they also had "the strength and suppleness of the pole-vaulter, the sprinter's speed, and the stamina of the long-distance runner—all needed in Balanchine's go-go ballets. They're a technicolor company, bright, vivid, exuberant and what they project, instead of temperament, is vitality and a zest for dancing, a sense of being in their element, which makes even those fiendishly difficult ballets look easy."

Balanchine has also concerned himself with destroying the "sissy image" of male dancers. One of the things he has done is to create strong roles for male stars, such as the lead in *Stars and Stripes,* for Jacques d'Amboise. Another product of the School of American Ballet, d'Amboise joined the New York City Ballet when he was fifteen, and *The New York Times* has called him "the first great American male dancer."

D'Amboise is a vibrant man, excited about his craft. But what excites him as much as dancing is choreography. He is one of a half dozen New York City Ballet dancers who have created ballets of their own. As must be expected, the Balanchine stamp is strong on d'Amboise, as it is on the others. There is an axiom that choreography cannot be taught, but it can be learned.

D'Amboise's first effort in 1960 was a fantasy of terror about a sleeping dancer waking to find his room crawling with weird-looking invaders. John Martin, then dance critic of *The New York*

Times, said of d'Amboise as choreographer, "Our bouncing boy has grown up." Since then d'Amboise has done other ballets, and another *Times* critic wrote, "Mr. d'Amboise, a strong dancer himself, creates gratefully for dancers."

Edward Villella is another of the strong New York City Ballet dancers who is creating new ballets, including one set to Prokofiev's Violin Concerto Number One. It was Prokofiev whose music was the background for *The Prodigal Son,* the ballet in which Villella scored his greatest triumph.

The youngest of the six home-grown choreographers, who was only recently old enough to vote, is John Clifford. He made his choreographic debut in 1968 with *Stravinsky Symphony* and has been choreographing ever since.

"I always wanted to make people move on the stage but I used to try and set bits of movement in the background that only ended up confusing the stage picture," Clifford explained. "I was choreographing selectively as if for a camera. I didn't realize that in the theater the spectator has to have a central focus because he's stationary; he can't move around like a camera picking up this and that.

Clifford doesn't read music, doesn't even have a record player. Whatever he likes, he mentally files away, and it seems to come out when he wants it.

"When I'm making a piece, I don't try to get the dancers to consciously project a meaning. I don't tell them what they're supposed to do except over coffee. Ideally, you just want the dancer to be. You try to get the ones you know will look right for the part in the first place and then things happen."

Balanchine constantly encourages his dancers to act on their desires to choreograph, because he feels the company must have its own creative continuity. But when Bernard Taper asked him, "What will happen to repertory after you go?" Balanchine said simply, "Who's going? I'm a Georgian. I expect to live to be 135."

During the twenty-week repertory ballet season at the State Theater, the company cost is estimated at more than $100,000 a week, a total of $2 million a year. Much of this is paid for by ticket sales, but in 1963 the Ford Foundation helped with a grant of $2 million to be spread out over a ten-year period.

An obvious expense is costumes, and the marvel is that Madame Karinska has done so much with so little. Of Karinska, Balanchine has said, "There is Shakespeare for literature and Madame Karinska for costumes." Critic Walter Terry added, "She does not clothe a body, nor simply dress it. Rather does she address herself to the task of making the garment a part of dancing itself." Madame Karinska described her work in terms of constructing a building: "The foundation is the important thing. In a costume, the foundation is the waist and you build up and down from there." The talent to translate the painter's sketch into fabric is a rare gift, but even rarer is Madame Karinska's ability to improvise so well with such a minimal budget.

Another major expense, of course, is for shoes. A single pair of shoes (at nine dollars a pair) can wear out in one performance. And a dancer can easily go through six to ten pairs a week.

Dancers consider their shoes as part of their body. They stretch tight shoes by dousing them in alcohol and dancing in them wet; they sew on strips of elastic to fit around the ankle; they cut off the satin from the toes, because it can split open after a few pirouettes, and prove dangerous during a performance. The "box" of the shoe is the hard part in the construction of the toe: There are also different methods of breaking in new shoes. Some dancers squeeze the box to soften it, but others use a hammer or even slam their locker door on it once or twice. Some also bang the toe of a new shoe on the floor to deaden the noise it produces.

The final attention to their shoes comes just before the dancers go on stage. They tie up the ribbons, often clipping them a little shorter and wetting the ends to keep them tightly tucked in. Then they work the toes of their shoes into a box of resin, rub some resin on the heels for better gripping, then dip the shoes and their tights into a bucket of water. As the water evaporates, the

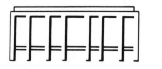

fabric in the heel of the shoe tightens and prevents slipping during the dance.

Ballet dancers never stop making changes in the shoes they wear, and some dancers change the design two or three times a year. "For one thing, your foot changes," said Suki Shorer. "Perhaps it gets stronger as you mature, and you decide you want less support and more flexibility." The Ballet Company also has a special fund it calls, "The Ballet Society Fund for the Care of Bunions and Corns"—for two chiropodists who handle all the dancers' foot problems.

But the dancers handle their own omens. Some are happy when they prick their fingers while sewing on the shoe ribbons. They carefully deposit a drop of blood inside the sole of each shoe, and this makes them feel that they'll give a better performance than usual. Others wish each other luck by using two fingers to signify devil's horns or occasionally they encourage one another before a performance with the theatrical classic, "Break a leg."

Once on stage, something almost chemical happens to the ballet dancer. Forgotten are the merciless exercises, the pain and fatigue, the ulcerated corns and the soft blisters. The actual performance provides a shock to the nervous system. On come the stage smiles, the enormous exhilaration, the clear excitement of body in motion.

For most of the performers, dance is a dedication. Gloria Govrin once left dancing to work as a receptionist for an insurance company. But when the season started, she found herself going to see the ballet every night. "What a corny scene I pulled when I quit the insurance company. I remember standing there saying, 'I've discovered that I have to dance.' "

The dancers come off the stage, drenched with sweat, their faces tense with strain, breathing hard, ready to collapse. "Sick, sick, sick," said Patricia McBride, after a draining performance in *Jewels*. Later, she relaxed and said, "When you make an exit, you die a little," adding, "I'm a shy person. Onstage I come to life. It's such a great feeling." Or as Melissa Hayden emphasized, "This is what my body is trained for."

Miss McBride began ballet lessons in New Jersey at the age of seven, joined the New York City Ballet at sixteen, started as a soloist the following year and became a principal dancer only a year later. A *New York Times* reviewer wrote, "If diamonds could dance, they would look like Patricia McBride." Melissa Hayden, who has a remarkable versatility with a repertoire of almost sixty ballets, has been called one of the great ballerinas of the world. Clive Barnes, Dance and Drama Critic of *The New York Times*, wrote: "American ballet is not so constructed as to have a prima ballerina assoluta but if it were, it would right now be Melissa Hayden. She is dancing with a kind of unquestioned authority that should make the birds sing on their branches."

In discussing the individual dancer, Edward Villella explained, "The company is bigger than any one dancer, it's a company in the fullest sense. I've been away and never been missed. The extraordinary thing about this company is that dancers are listed in alphabetical order and any role can be covered by other dancers."

About the company's female dancers, Nicholas Magallanes said, "Each of them is technically able to be a top ballerina anywhere else. They have the rare combination of youth and polish. They're the cream."

Magallanes himself, like most of the others, came out of Balanchine's School of American Ballet. "With all of us, rehearsal time is always," he continued. "You can suddenly do one thing, and then all the practice, all the fifth positions are worthwhile—but only you may know it."

"A dancer is first of all an animal," Balanchine tells them. "Animal is lazy. Existence is a struggle. No animal is going to run like mad unless he has a reason. A lion only runs when it's hungry to catch something. A race horse won't run if it has no jockey. Who do you want to go to for dance? A doctor? He'll give you milk of magnesia. Why come here? To improve, to form right habits, to force the body, to feel pain. And not to do something good once but four times until you're exhausted and then it's good."

Balanchine gives priority to his dancers, no matter who else or what else is waiting. He is usually backstage before the first dancer arrives and after the last one leaves. During one intermission a dancer requested advice on improving a specific motion, and immediately Balanchine was oblivious to all else, concentrating completely on her.

"This is his family," said staff member Virginia Donaldson. "And this is his home."

Balanchine dancers know they're good, and they prove it more often than any other company in the world. Their 216 performances in 33 weeks are almost twice as many as Russia's famous Bolshoi Ballet or England's Royal Ballet. And while the Bolshoi and the Royal stick closely to the standard ballets with the principal dancers performing the familiar roles, the New York City Ballet is constantly rehearsing new ballets and maintains an active repertory of at least fifty works.

Peter Martins, a principal dancer with the Royal Danish Ballet, was invited by Balanchine to be a guest artist with the New York City Ballet during the 1968-69 season. "In Denmark we have fewer ballets and they are more traditional, with older dancers," he commented. "But this New York City Ballet is such a young ballet company, so much more exciting, always reaching and stretching its excitement."

And there are still the holiday-season performances of *The Nutcracker*, primarily for children of all ages. During a recent season Richard Clurman, Chairman of the Board of City Center and a member of the Lincoln Center Board, took 5,000 of the highly prized tickets for *The Nutcracker* and had them distributed to ghetto children, almost all of whom had never seen a ballet before. And the children weren't grouped in any corner of the State Theater—their seats were sprinkled throughout the house. For the children it was a memorable evening; for Richard Clurman it was a small sample of many more such things to come.

"Balanchine is a genius," Clurman said. "His is the gift of creating beauty. My job is to make that beauty of ballet and of the New York City Opera reach deep into the lives of the many, not just the few. Otherwise it just isn't fair."

Mme. Sophie Pourmel, whose title for many years has been "Supervisor of Women's Wardrobe," has a full memory record of the beauty and excitement of the New York City Ballet. Her sentiments echo Clurman's: "First the ballet belongs to Balanchine because it comes out of his magic. Then it belongs to the dancers because it comes out of their sweat and their talent. But, most of all, it must belong to the people because this hunger for beauty comes out of their need."

NEW YORK CITY OPERA

"We are not competing with the Met. We are different in our ideological outlook, our feeling for what opera is about, and we achieve different results." —Julius Rudel, Director of the New York City Opera

The box at the State Theater was crowded with City Opera singers watching their associates in a new production. At the end of a scene sung with particular brilliance, everyone in the box cheered "Bravo" so enthusiastically that a staff member had to hush them, saying, "You better stop. The audience will think you're a hired claque."

That's just a small illustration of the special spirit of the New York City Opera. It is not the youngest opera group in the world—it has already had its twenty-fifth birthday—but it still has many of the characteristics of a young group: an eagerness to try new things; a real intimacy among its people; the constant challenge of operating on a slim budget.

The New York City Opera budget, of course, is not as slim as it was a decade ago at the Mecca Temple. It has been helped by Ford Foundation money, strengthened by the Lincoln Center address and buttressed by a reputation that has reached around the world. But the City Opera is still a deficit operation, like every other constituent at the Center, and its existence is a constant struggle.

The New York City Opera did not have an easy entry into Lincoln Center. The Board was fully in favor of bringing in the New York City Ballet, but it already had the great and glamorous Metropolitan, so why, many asked, have another opera company? Still, there were strong arguments in its favor: The City Opera catered to a different audience on a different price level, and it had a highly individual approach towards the type of

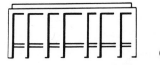

opera it wanted to produce. The final ruling came from New York State, which financed the State Theater and decreed that the New York City Opera must be admitted, along with the Ballet. With some reluctance the Met and other members of the Board agreed.

In contrast to the Met, which had a rather rigid star system, the New York City Opera originally favored the ensemble group idea. That concept encourages interchanging singers in various roles. Gradually, however, the City Opera evolved its own star system, but with a major difference: The Met hired top singing stars from all over the world; the New York City Opera developed its own stars.

Even more important, however, is its unique approach to opera.

"To us the extraordinary and exciting thing about opera is that it can be made meaningful on many levels to people of varied backgrounds," emphasized Julius Rudel, Director of the City Opera. "We don't just conjure up kings and queens from a musical museum; we want to produce operas that democratize people."

It was Noel Coward who once proclaimed, "The trouble with opera is not that it isn't what it used to be, but that it is." Rudel disagrees. "Opera changes as much as our whole culture changes," he said. "It's a continuing process. It is trying to find itself, but it's too early to write it off. We go on the basic belief that opera is alive."

More than any other director in this country, Rudel has proven the point again and again.

In most of the grand opera houses of the world, the repertory has generally shrunk to some fifty "authenticated" masterpieces. Many great singers, so much in demand—particularly because of the multiplicity of recordings and television appearances—have felt it unnecessary to learn new roles. Staggering costs have made new productions seem like huge gambles. Anthony A. Bliss, former President of the Metropolitan Opera Association, once declared, "Opera is a 16th-century art to which we are trying to apply 20th-century economics." Any production must be amortized over a long period because its costs can add up to six figures, covering such items as costumes, scenery, artists' fees, stagehands'

payrolls, rehearsal time, administrative service, storage and building expenses. Estimates indicate that each new opera must initially run for a minimum of eighteen performances to even partly pay for itself.

British critic Peter Hayworth feels that this enormous expense has accentuated the museum concept of opera and warns that as a result "the alienation between opera and the outside world takes on a new and more sinister dimension. For the movement that started by driving the broad public out of the opera house had ended by evicting the composer as well."

In defense Rudolf Bing answered, "We [the Metropolitan Opera Company] are entrusted with the works it has taken 300 years of genius to create. . . . The Metropolitan Museum of Art is not attacked because it doesn't show Chagalls." Modern works, he pointed out, appear in the Museum of Modern Art.

In relation to the Met, Julius Rudel's New York City Opera is opera's Museum of Modern Art. Rudel has no interest in "grand" as it pertains to opera. City Opera does produce some of the "bread and butter" classics and even occasionally goes in for pomp and lavish spectacle. "But we try to look at all the old operas in a new light, to see what we can discover to make them meaningful in our day," he noted. "When we redid *Faust*, we did it in a way which pointed up the basic drama, the very essence of the inside of the work, rather than the beautiful outside trimmings. We tried to discover the same kind of fresh meaning in *Julius Caesar*. Of course, we try to take a fresh approach to the music, too."

Rudel is keenly aware that many of America's most respected composers have shied away from opera, partly because there are so few places for exposure. So he himself has searched out, commissioned and presented some forty American operas—besides a host of new works by foreign composers. His emphasis is based on his vision of opera as exciting theater.

Opera always has been exciting theater for Rudel. He was just out of school and only twenty-one years old when he persuaded the brand-new City Center to hire him as their first rehearsal pianist. He worked without salary for almost six months but they finally gave him fifty dollars. "I was upset, naturally," Rudel remembered. "I went to the house director and complained. So he gave me another ten dollars." Rudel was only twenty-three when in 1945 he got his chance to conduct at City Center for the final performance of *The Gypsy Baron*. "I had to walk into the pit cold, but after that I got crumbs from the table now and then."

The crumbs soon increased in quantity and quality. Rudel started directing the offstage choruses and solos that mesh with the stage action and orchestra, prompting singers onstage for their entrances and substituting for conductors at ensemble rehearsals. Finally he even took on the supreme headache of organizing rehearsal schedules, which meant keeping everybody simultaneously at work on different phases of a dozen operas. That demanded an intimate knowledge of the repertoire, as well as the quirks and capabilities of all the personalities, and the almost-military logistics of stage coordination.

But by 1956 the City Opera had gone through three directors and a series of crises, and was nearly bankrupt. The decision had been made to kill the spring season of 1957, and there was considerable talk about converting City Center into a parking garage. It was then that members of the cast and company got together—without consulting Rudel—and proposed him as the man to direct the New York City Opera.

Several nights later Rudel got a call from Newbold Morris, Chairman of the Board. "What are you doing?" asked Morris. "I'm going to *Inherit the Wind*," replied Rudel. The Chairman of the Board laughed, "You already have," he told Rudel, and offered him the job of Director.

The company's first director, Laszlo Halasz, (1943-51) was the more emotional type, and so were his immediate successors, Joseph Rosenstack (1952-56) and Erich Leinsdorf (the fall of 1956). Not Rudel. He's generally a quiet man. "I don't know whether Julius really lacks the exhibitionism of the average conductor or whether he is just a lot brighter than most conductors," reported one of his associates. "If you praise him, he'll pretend that he's nobody at all and point out what a fine bunch of artists, or what a fine chorus, or what a

fine orchestra he has to work with. That attitude, of course, makes the artists feel great, and they all break their backs to do their best. So he gets a fine performance—a better one, most of the time, than a yelling despot would get."

Another reason Rudel can develop this company closeness more easily is because he is not only the director but a conductor as well. He is still part and parcel of every production, from its preliminary discussion to its final rehearsal. When the company works late, he works late with them. When feelings are ruffled, he is there to soothe them.

Rudel's innovations have been artistic and managerial, as well as personal. Helped by a Ford grant, he put on a season of American opera each spring for three years. "The idea" he said, "was to convince the public that American operatic writing had come of age. To convince myself that this was so, I looked through about 200 scores and eventually came up with an initial 20 operas. We lost a great deal of money, but we did persuade people that a lot of American composers were worth listening to. Out of those years came, *The Ballad of Baby Doe*, *The Crucible*, *Good Soldier Schweik* and *Six Characters*—some of which are still in our repertory." Rudel then brought in the best contemporary opera from abroad: Prokofiev, Britten, Poulenc, Shostakovich, Stravinsky and Strauss.

The New York City Opera's move to the State Theater represented no change in style, tone or direction. The move did mean an enormous increase in comfort for the cast, but it also confronted the technicians with a challenge. The State Theater was originally conceived as a home for Dance, not Opera.

At first, "The acoustics were miserable—in fact, absolutely impossible," related Technical Director Hans Sondheimer. "I remember one woman in the audience writing us a letter, saying, '. . . the singer was on stage right and we heard the sound coming from stage left. . . .' It was even worse than that. Two people could sit in seats next to each other and one would hear everything perfectly and the other person might hardly hear it at all. The distribution of sound was very uneven. Echoes would bounce back all over

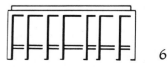

the place. The ceiling wasn't designed in the right shape to deflect sound. And the hall was full of plaster instead of wood, and there was lots of metal which made the sound very crisp. But I swore we would never use amplification for voice reinforcement, and we never did. Amplification and opera do not mix.

"We did all kinds of things to improve the acoustics. We placed large reflecting baffles on the rear wall of the stage to accomplish more even distribution of sound all over the house, and we installed baffles and velour panels all around the walls in the auditorium to eliminate disturbing reverberation and peculiar echoes. We threw out some panels of glass and put down some extra carpets in the passageways of the rings. Now we have an opera house where you can really hear the good sound of opera."

But Sondheimer lives with other daily challenges. If the Met is highly mechanized, the City Opera is highly improvised. And Sondheimer's technical staff is one-third the size of the Met's. There are no pushbuttons to manipulate the one hundred pipes on which the scenery hangs—everything is manual. Nor has he any facilities to build his own props or sets. And since there are no mechanical wagons to move sets on stage, all scenery has to be built in multiples (four-by-eight) so it can be more easily moved and stored. A further complication is that the door to the freight elevator is nine feet high and twenty feet long, and any scenery that doesn't fit into that elevator has to be cut apart Sondheimer tries to plan his props so that many are collapsible, but there are such things as sixteen-foot towers for *Julius Caesar* that refuse to fit any formula. He must even share storage space with the State Theater's two other tenants, the Ballet and the Music Theater.

Sondheimer could help change the sound and redesign the scenery but what could he do about the plain floor stage? If he needed a trapdoor, he had to have a hole cut into the floor. And the floor vibrated when it was jumped on. The stage, after all, had been designed for dancers.

The State Theater also offers its challenge to J. Edgar Joseph, or "Edgar," as he's known in the Company. Edgar is City Opera's "Costumer"; he supervises everything in a single room and often works alone.

"We put on fourteen operas in less than nine weeks," he said, "and that's one reason we have a great family feeling. That's why everybody calls me 'Edgar.' I would say sixty percent of the people in the Company call the Director by his first name. There's a real closeness here, and especially in my department. When singers come to me for a fitting and take their clothes off, they very often take the shades off their minds, too. They're far more relaxed and say a lot more than they might ordinarily say, and you get a real insight into their feelings.

"And you quickly find out which of the two schools of singers they belong to: the school of singers that likes a tight voice, to give something to push against; or the school of singers that likes a loose voice, so they can expand inside. Once you find out which school they belong to, then you know whether to take the waist in, or leave it like a sack." According to Edgar, the one requirement all singers have in common is that there be no piece of costume clothing within eight inches of the larynx. "There's a little hollow underneath the larynx, and they can feel the pressure of anything near it and then they just can't sing," he said.

Most of the City Opera singers are younger than those at the Met so their costumes require more alterations. "Their rib cages keep growing and changing," Edgar noted, "and they develop stronger diaphragms, more muscle. And this means, bless their hearts, they come in here singing better. It's easy to let their clothes out a little on the side. But we also have great variations in weight, particularly in the chorus, and sometimes we let them know that there's no more material in their costume to be let out. They get the hint and start dieting. We have a very weight-conscious company. And we encourage them. We have one very heavy girl in the company who lost something like forty pounds in ten weeks. She's a beautiful girl, and we're delighted when she comes in to tell us that her costumes are getting too big and need taking in."

The Plaza Fountain

The Metropolitan Opera House

The Magic Flute, designed for the Metropolitan Opera by Marc Chagall: stage curtain, . . .

and "The Animal Scene"

Die Walküre, directed and conducted at the
Metropolitan Opera by Herbert von Karajan, with
Thomas Stewart as Wotan and Birgit Nilsson
as Brünnhilde

Aïda, above, designed by Robert O'Hearn; and
Falstaff, directed at the Metropolitan Opera by
Franco Zeffirelli

A New York Philharmonic Promenades concert,
conducted by André Kostelanetz

The Vivian Beaumont Theater

Shakespeare's *King Lear* with Lee J. Cobb
as Lear, Philip Bosco (left), as Kent, and Rene
Auberjonois as the Fool

Molière's *The Miser* with Robert Symonds as Harpagon

William Gibson's *A Cry of Players*, with Anne Bancroft as Anne, Frank Langella as Will, and Jackie Paris as Susanna

George Balanchine's *Symphony in C,* with Suki
Schorer and Deni Lamont

George Balanchine's *Ballet Imperial*, with
Jacques d'Amboise

Julius Rudel, Director of the New York City Opera

The New York City Opera production of *Le Coq
d'Or*, with Beverly Sills as Queen Shemakha and
Norman Treigle as King Dodon

LINCOLN CENTER
FOR THE PERFORMING ARTS

PHILHARMONIC HALL
OPENING SEPTEMBER 23, 1962

In order of appearance, posters on the following pages by Ben Shahn, Frank Stella, Allan D'Arcangelo, Robert Indiana, Elsworth Kelly, Larry Rivers, Saul Bass, Andy Warhol, Roy Lichtenstein. All posters commissioned by Lincoln Center for the Performing Arts, Inc., through List Art Posters.

VIVIAN BEAUMONT THEATER
LINCOLN CENTER   1965

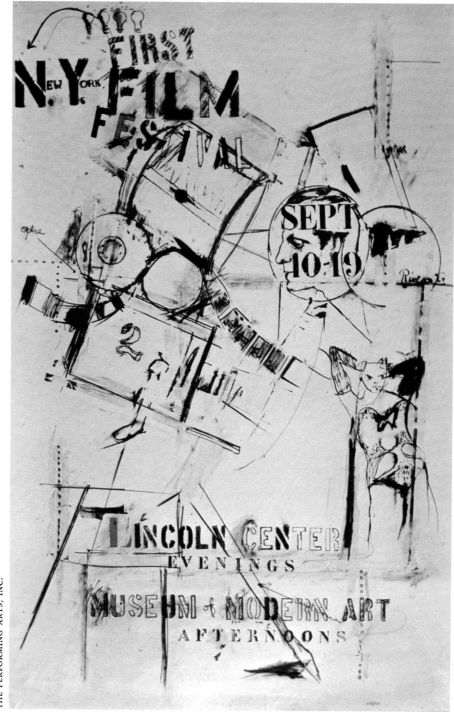

PHOTOGRAPH BY BOB SERATING, A LIST ART POSTER COURTESY OF LINCOLN CENTER FOR THE PERFORMING ARTS, INC.

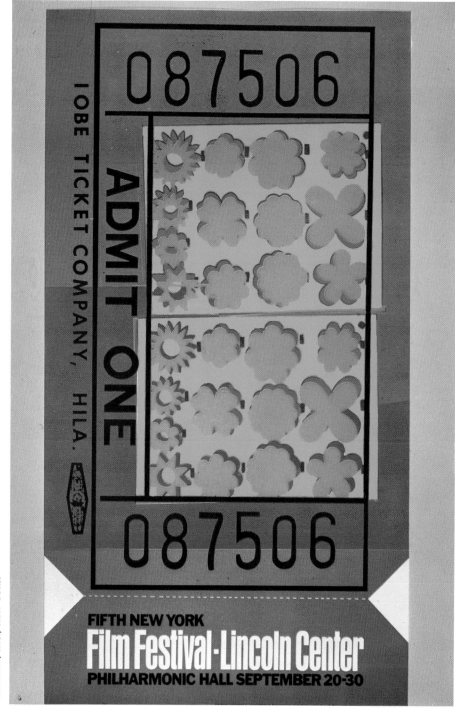

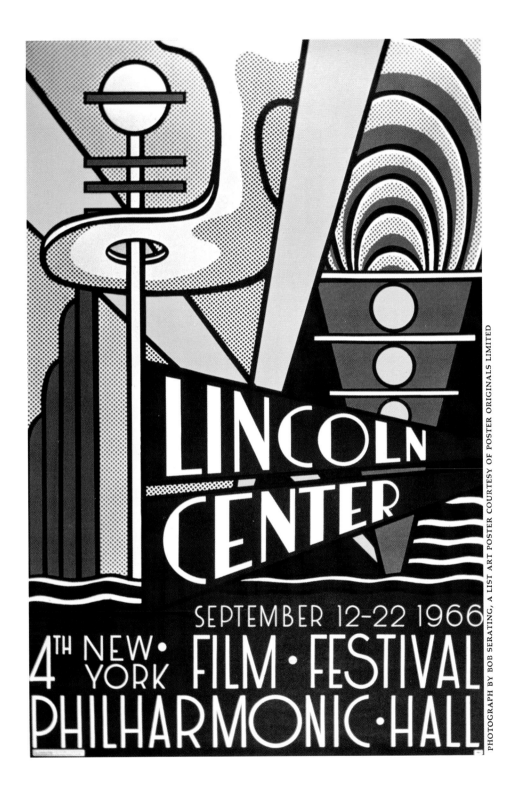

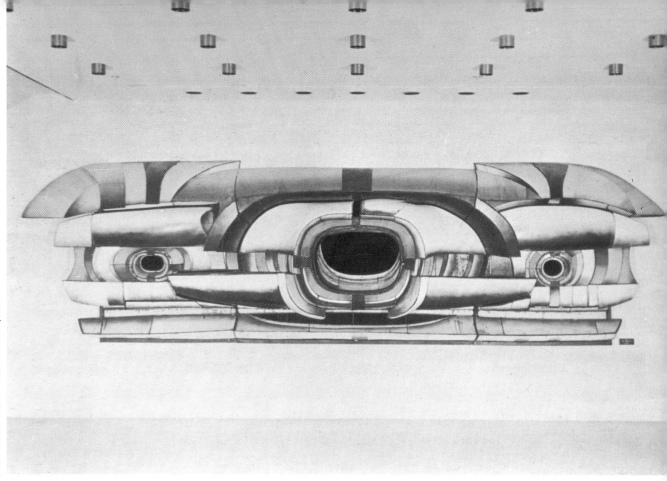

"Untitled Relief, 1964" by Lee Bontecou,
New York State Theater

"Orpheus and Apollo" by Richard Lippold,
Philharmonic Hall

"Le Guichet" by Alexander Calder,
Lincoln Center Plaza

"K. 458, The Hunt" by Dimitri Hadzi,
Philharmonic Hall

The Plaza Fountain, and a Lincoln Center Guided Tour

The Library & Museum of the Performing Arts:
The Children's Library and the Main Reading Room

The Juilliard School

A private instruction studio at Juilliard

The completed Lincoln Center

Philharmonic Hall

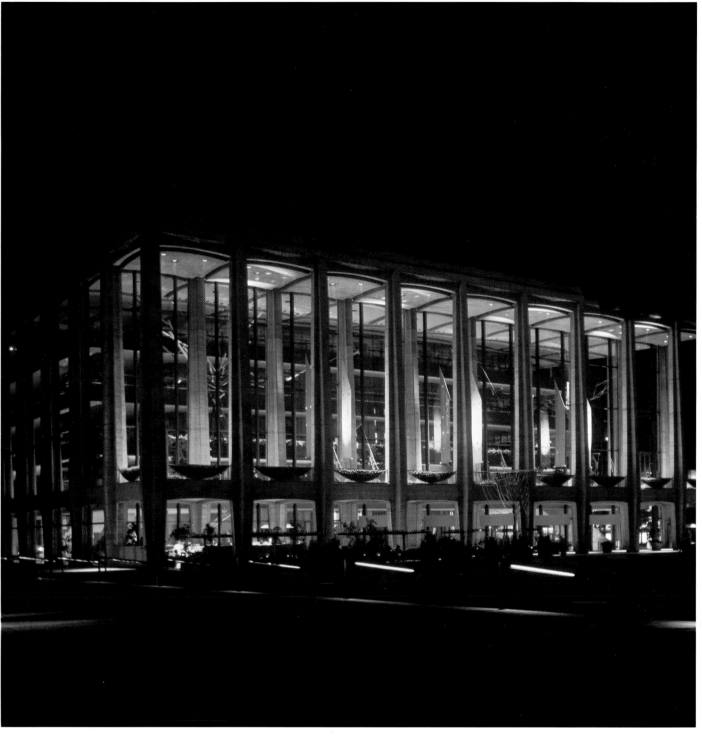

Philharmonic Hall decorated for the Promenades
concerts.

Edgar and his small staff eagerly expropriate costumes from old operas for new operas—as long as the fabric is there, and whole, not falling apart, and provided it's the right color. "We also do quite a bit of our own dyeing here, which saves money. And we have our own washing machine and dryer. For a new production, we must go through our stock and find out what the designer will accept. For *Igor*, we have probably 80 to 100 costumes in the house which, with alterations, dyeing, or something, can be used. *Igor* is made up primarily of Russian peasants. Everybody knows Russian peasants wear a blouse, a pair of bloomers and boots. All that's needed is the right color pattern, a basic shape, and some very distinctive hats. I've got a wardrobe man who's fantastic with hats, if he ever has time."

Edgar and his staff make about thirty percent of the costumes. "The greatest friends we have own a costume house and they love opera and they love us and we love them, and I don't think they make much money on us. When we ask them for real leather, we get real leather, and when we request gold trim, we get gold trim."

The fact that a fabric house enters into the family feeling of City Opera is not surprising. It is yet another example of the enormous spirit of closeness that prevails in the Company. This is also one opera company that doesn't even have a prompter. "If you have to rely on a man in a little lighted box to give the cues, then spontaneity goes right out the window," said Julius Rudel. "You gain security at the expense of communicating directly with the audience."

This direct communication sometimes causes problems. In the first act of *Bomarzo*, a fog is supposed to envelop the entire stage. During one performance the fog blew into the orchestra pit and neither the musicians nor the singers could see the conductor for direction. Rudel somehow managed to keep things going.

"I can often sense when something is about to happen," he commented. "You can see it in the eyes of a singer or instrumentalist. You may have to give a cue, adjust the tempo to provide time for an extra breath, or slow down to accommodate some unexpected piece of stage action. One year a tenor forgot the French words to his big aria in Act Two of *Manon*. He made up several lines in some sort of esperanto and then I gave him a clear cue in French. He looked blankly at me for a moment, and suddenly, he remembered everything. On another occasion a young soprano who was making her debut as 'Butterfly' got lost during the second act. She stopped, walked down to the footlights and said, 'I'm sorry, maestro.' I smiled as encouragingly as I could and nodded to the other singer on stage whose next line, most appropriately was 'Quanta Pieta.' To my relief, the girl recovered and finished the performance."

City Opera programming is influenced not only by what they are able to cast, but by what other opera houses are *not* doing. Since, for example, there is so much Verdi produced everywhere, City Opera does not feel impelled to do all his popular works. It may be the only opera company in the world that has done more Menotti than Verdi.

The New York City Opera is willing to try almost anything, but avant-garde composers currently seem to offer only limited promise. "They have done extraordinary things with the voice—distorting it with tapes and bull-horns—but they still have to concern themselves with the stage," Rudel explained. "One of the difficulties of American avant-garde music is that it is so firmly attached to university life and the rather inbred audiences that are found there, and therefore it's isolated from the real world of real audiences.

"On the other hand, you have a man like Ginastera, who is dramatically descended from Verdi. He is able to extend the legitimate use of musical instruments and voices in highly original ways and still keep his audience interested."

Bomarzo, Alberto Ginastera's most controversial work, is the story of a highly personal, shocking nightmare. In a complex of hallucination and reality, the dying Duke of Bomarzo looks back over his whole life. The emotions of all the other characters are seen through the Duke's imagination.

Bomarzo's music is contemporary, its plot complicated and lurid. There was much critical

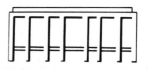

acclaim for the director, Tito Capobianco, for creating the mood and for being its architect as well as its interpreter.

"The secret of being a director is that you have to kill yourself to show the artists that you know the opera better than they do," Capobianco said. "Creation comes from one brain—the rest is collaboration. An artist, for example, sees only a partial picture of the opera with himself as the center of it. The director has to put the whole work in perspective."

Capobianco has staged some sixty operas. His planning is meticulous, and rehearsals never start until he has plotted the last detail of a production's design and movement. "In art, I am not democratic," he insisted.

Capobianco was also largely responsible for the dramatic conviction of three more of City Opera's most sparkling hits: *Don Rodrigo*, (also by Ginastera), Handel's *Julius Caesar* and Massenet's *Manon*. In addition to his work at the City Opera, Capobianco later became Director of the American Opera Theater at the Juilliard School.

Frank Corsaro, stage director of the New York City Opera, similiarly typifies the City Opera style of giving old operas a lively new look. Discussing Corsaro's direction of *Cavalleria Rusticana* and *Pagliacci*, music critic Donald Delany wrote, "It was almost like seeing these old favorites for the first time. The characters are no longer singers going through the motion of playing parts. They act and look like flesh-and-blood people. Rarely does anyone stand around motionless during an aria. Instead the singers go about bits of 'business' which are, for the most part, so natural that one wonders why nobody thought of them before."

Corsaro comes to opera by way of television and Broadway. "As far as my work is concerned, Broadway and opera enrich each other," he explained. "Too many opera companies update a classic opera simply by giving it a new set. At City Opera, we try to approach the old opera with a fresh concept, make it more modern.

"I've just read of a *Carmen* set in a discotheque and an *Aïda* amidst a war between the Israelis and the Arabs. Giving opera its present lead, we will yet see a topless *Aïda*." Corsaro firmly believes that the stage director must be willing to take chances. "Convention is his nemesis. He must take nothing for granted.

"I don't even think we've rendered Mozart properly—or improperly enough," he continued. "Mozart is a subtle humanist, and yet to watch most productions of *Figaro, Cosi fan tutte* or *Don Giovanni*, you'd think he was Mr. Buffo Buffonissimo himself. A straighter, actually more realistic approach would reveal the fantastic humanity pleading to assert itself through all the mannered nonsense passing as Mozartian style today. A director should stress greater logic— moment to moment—in developing Mozart's schemes. What appears arbitrary or implausible in the libretto has an unerring logic when viewed in the proper perspective. The director must find the thread and weave it."

At one time opera stage directors were not considered very important. In the original production of *Madame Butterfly* at La Scala in 1904, the stage director wasn't even credited on the program, although almost everyone else was. Nowadays, however, the director is regarded as a kind of artistic god.

"The marvelous thing about repertory opera is that we can keep changing an opera if we want to," Corsaro noted, referring to changes in staging after the first performance. "But if we now have a repertory opera, we also have an aware repertory audience. If I make some change in an opera, I often have somebody stop me outside the stage door or write me a letter asking why I did it. I think that's absolutely wonderful.

"The art of arriving at basic decisions regarding dramatic necessity versus musical necessity is a fantastic business. Dealing with musical masterpieces is like dealing with life-blood itself —the thing being re-created from scratch! Sometimes, as I work, I feel that I'm decoding. At the end of Act I in my production of *La Traviata*, I asked Violetta to take a long, long pause before launching into *E strano*. The conductor and I argued endlessly about it. How long should the pause be? And why? I only knew that it was an important private moment for Violetta, a pause to recover from the fatigue of her 'party manner' and illness before being forced to resume her false gaiety. This is drama at a point which usually comes off as a 'concert piece' with the soprano stepping in to sing a song and leaving all dramatic logic behind her."

Basically Corsaro doesn't believe in gimmicks. In reshaping Gounod's *Faust*, he was more concerned with the core of the work than he was with its facade.

"We're trying for a sensual quality," he told his performers at rehearsal, "otherwise it's clutch-and-grab all the way."

A great many singers generally agree that a good director is the basic force that creates a unity between performer and role. Problems come when the singer's conception collides with the director's. "If a director is a dictator and unable to listen to anyone else, he's not a director but a traffic cop," Norman Treigle commented.

Frank Corsaro is not a traffic cop. He knows what he wants, but he can listen. When he restaged *Faust*, he listened to Norman Treigle, the gaunt-looking man who for almost fifteen years had been playing Mephistopheles magnificently— with exquisite timing, sureness and high theatricality. The *Variety* critic called his performance "so good he had to seem unbelievable." The role had become a part of Treigle. "You know it like you know yourself," he said. "And Frank accepted my concept of Mephistopheles and practically everything I've refined it down to."

Treigle indicated, however, that he doesn't come to rehearsals with the "I-know-my-role-and-this-is-it" approach. "I try to prepare myself by being ready to respond, by being adaptable. I try not to get involved in a role during the rehearsal period—rehearsal is for setting things, for trying this, discarding that. If you're involved in the thing, how can you make those decisions? You have to be calm for that. Besides, it's the performance that should get your effort. It's like being in college—the exam is the performance. Rehearsal is just study."

Treigle moves from baritone to bass with equal effectiveness. His voice is capable of great variety and color, and it can produce such immense volume as to seem almost unrestrained. But "star" in opera means more than a big voice;

it also means personality, acting, projection—all mixed with a kind of magic.

"I don't think the talent of being able to charge a stage with electricity is anything that can be acquired" Treigle added. "You must be onstage for a purpose: to give to the audience. And when I get in front of an audience—I don't know, I light up, that's all. Another thing, I never set anything vocally. The voice just has to come out of your response to the situation, to the words and music. I see people so worried about their vocal technique that they can't express anything. But the more you leave yourself open, the freer and better your singing will be."

Soprano Beverly Sills is the other super-star of the New York City Opera. She is now among the international elite of singers and has sung with virtually every leading opera company in the world, including La Scala. One of the few exceptions is the Metropolitan, where she had been invited to sing but could not reach agreement on repertoire. "But *this* is my company," she said of the New York City Opera. "My career was built in this opera house. I love working with Julius Rudel."

This young, Brooklyn-born woman with the warm, wonderful voice made her debut at City Center in 1955. "It was an impossible house to sing in. The acoustics were terrible. It was like a big barn, dirty and dusty, and from the stage you looked out on that vast nothingness. I used to feel that I was in a movie house, a vaudeville actor between the double feature." Sills was delighted when they moved to the State Theater—even though she missed having windows in her dressing room.

But her success still did not come overnight. "Singers have made careers with ten roles," she recalled. "I had to learn a hundred. For years I covered other singers in their roles. It wasn't like the movies where you see the understudy getting her big chance. Nobody I covered ever got sick."

The Beverly Sills skyrocket really took off in 1966 when she sang Cleopatra in Handel's *Julius Caesar*. It was a coloratura showcase and she was as ready as a polished diamond, singing the difficult arias with clarity and color and with an almost effortless ease and purity. *Newsweek* critic

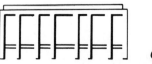

Hubert Saal, wrote, "Her coloratura is unmatched by anyone's. Not only is it remarkably flexible, incredibly quick and perfectly true, but the florid notes are crystal-clear, variable in color even at such altitudes and speeds, and full-bodied, taking part in the drama of the opera rather than being mere exhibitions of agility."

Sills at her summit is an unpretentious prima donna, and Rudel is committed to keeping her happy. After her success with *Julius Caesar*, the two had lunch, and Sills remembered that Rudel asked her "What do you want to do next?"

"It so happened I asked for *Manon*, which is a passion with Rudel. He loves to conduct it, so what I asked was a gift for both of us, really. He got so excited that within five minutes after I said the word *Manon*, we had agreed on the tenor, the designer, the director and even where the money was going to come from! By the same token, he chose *Le Coq d'Or*; I never would have requested it, because I'm not by nature a dancer, never wiggle my hips. But Julius brought it up, thinking it would be comic relief after *Manon* and *Julius Caesar*, saying, 'Why not be funny?' So I had a ball with that.

"*Lucia* I did ask for. For one thing, we'd never done it, and I felt we had the voices. We did it with a great deal of integrity, and we did it uncut —showed the whole opera for what it really is, rather than as just a coloratura showcase. I think that's why we've had this enormous acclaim, because now *Lucia* is not just a tweet-tweet birdy part, but a real tragic character. By omitting the cuts, the tenor stops being such a jerk and becomes quite interesting himself. And there's a scene with a bass, usually considered unimportant —anyone will do. But now he's become such a dominant character that the part was carefully chosen and given to a first-string bass. It's changed the whole character of the opera."

Despite the obvious fact that Treigle and Sills are stars of major magnitude, Rudel insists that "At all times we try to serve the work at hand. We're not interested in making it a vehicle for a star, a director or a designer. God knows we all have enough ego, but it is much healthier to want to display the work rather than oneself."

The artistic health of the New York City Opera is excellent. Everything about it has burgeoned. The basic orchestra has grown from 39 to 57. The twin seasons at the old City Center seldom totaled more than eleven weeks with 65 performances. The 1969-70 season was nineteen weeks with 150 performances, not counting the tours. From 65 percent of capacity, attendance has jumped to 96 percent.

"The shoestring days are over," remarked Managing Director John S. White. "The most expensive opera ever mounted in the old house was *Louise*, it cost $21,000. Our *Manon* here cost $160,000."

"But we're keeping our ticket prices down" insisted Norman Singer, Executive Director, City Center of Music and Dance, Inc. "Our basic keynote is quality, but we want to spread it around, make as much of it available to as many people as we can. That's the rock on which our concept is based."

With expenses up, prices still down and money harder to find, the City Opera has managed to keep its working schedule packed.

The busiest time of the year, of course, is early in the season when there are always four or five rehearsals in progress. The one man who always makes the rounds, poking his head into each rehearsal room, is Music Administrator Felix Popper. Popper still works as a conductor and coach, when he can find the time, and describes himself as a man "diseased with opera."

"I must be diseased," he said wryly. "Why else would I subject myself to such madness?"

What Popper means by madness is his responsibility for the preparation of all productions. This involves a working knowledge of more than a hundred operas and an ability to read an unfamiliar work and recognize all its requirements in terms of cast, chorus and orchestra. He must also, of course, know the rehearsal regulations of various unions, and have an infinite supply of flexible plans to cover any calamity from laryngitis to snowstorms.

Julius Rudel relies on Popper to sense potential problems before a crisis explodes.

"We begin by facing the fact that we're dealing with the impossible," noted Popper. "There simply isn't enough time or space. So our challenge is to maximize the effectiveness of every second we have. Everything has to be planned to the exact moment. If a rehearsal starts ten minutes after it's supposed to, it can set back the entire day."

To keep rehearsals properly paced, Popper checks them constantly. Progress reports are detailed on his coded master sheet. Among his constant conferences are those that deal with costumes, publicity, technical and directing problems and union negotiations. He also keeps a small black notebook in which he records his comments on company auditions for ambitious chorus members.

Such is the wonder of Felix Popper's compartmentalized mind that he somehow still manages to do coaching for three or four hours a day during the season. One of his friends tells the story of a new usher stopping Popper from entering an exit door after the curtain had dropped.

"I'm sorry," said the usher, "no one's allowed in the theater after the performance."

"It's all right," answered Popper calmly. "I live here."

That's the way it is with the New York City Opera company—they all live here.

THE MUSIC THEATER OF LINCOLN CENTER

"Lincoln Center may be Pagliacci to you, but it's Richard Rodgers to me." —Anonymous

The story of the Music Theater has been the story of one man—Richard Rodgers.

"The Music Theater was born because my good friend, Bill Schuman, asked my advice on what we could do to fill the empty State Theater in the summer," Rodgers reminisced. "And the Music Theater has filled it, better than we could have hoped."

The Music Theater is among the envied constituents of Lincoln Center because it actually makes some money. It can do that because it maintains no permanent company or staff. Broadway talent is always available when Rodgers is ready to present another musical. And

producer-director Rodgers also has no trouble acquainting himself with the plays—because most of them are his.

The Music Theater was inaugurated with *The King and I* in July, 1964, and since then has presented *Carousel, Annie Get Your Gun, South Pacific* and in 1969, *Oklahoma!* The non-Rodgers musicals have included *Show Boat, Kismet* and *The Merry Widow.*

"I'm happy to say that they all played to capacity houses," said Rodgers. "Bill and I did talk of producing new musicals, too, but our problem is the size of the State Theater. It's big. To pull in almost 2,800 people every night for something new is risky business. But there are smaller theaters in Lincoln Center like the Forum and the new Alice Tully Hall, and maybe we can use them for other ideas."

Rodgers noted that the Music Theater had sponsored the pioneering Exploratory Theater productions of *Berlin Is Mine* and *Dandelion Wine* at the Forum Theater. It also had produced the concert performances of "George Gershwin's Theater" and "Jerome Kern's Theater" at Philharmonic Hall.

"And whenever we put something on, we also draw some of our talent from Juilliard or the other groups here. I'm a Juilliard graduate myself. Anyway, even though we seem to be a floating constituent without real roots, we still have a real purpose."

Rodgers now has as his associate Goddard Lieberson, who has had impressive experience in theater, television and music. Lieberson has his own vision of the Music Theater's future: "I would like to see the Music Theater operate as a repertory theater like the Metropolitan Opera. The Met is a repertory museum of the great operas and we could be a repertory museum of the great American musicals—and the musical is our unique contribution to the theater of the world.

"But we don't have to compete with Broadway, and we shouldn't," Lieberson continued. "Ideally, we shouldn't even have to worry about being a commercial success. We should be able to present musicals that deserve to be seen again. And we shouldn't change them. We should play them straight. Musicals like

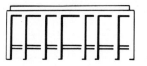

Girl Crazy, with all those great tunes, and *Oh Kay* and *No, No, Nanette*. Sure, their books aren't any good anymore, but you can say the same thing about the book of *La Boheme* or *Carmen*. The point is they will have a special quality, maybe a little campy now, but I know there will be a ready audience for them."

Lieberson thinks of this project as a "peephole into the past," but filled with the talent of the future—the young choreographers, the young singers, the young dancers—who would infuse those old musicals with their own freshness. He would like to see these musicals designed with simpler sets, smaller orchestras and staging that is more suggestive than spectacular. It's a formula that promises to leap over the generation gap.

That kind of impact was in evidence when during the 1969 season Lieberson produced a night of "The Heyday of Rodgers and Hart" on behalf of the Music Theater. Much of the audience had come to remember, and the mood of the evening was rich in nostalgia. But there was also a large sampling of young people, many of whom had perhaps come to listen for the first time. Ray Bolger proved again that his dancing grace was timeless; a film clip of Maurice Chevalier singing "Mimi" to a pouting Jeanette MacDonald was funny, campy and great; and Benny Goodman on the clarinet played with such style and magic that feet were beating in rhythm all over the hall, old feet along with young.

In keeping with his goals, Lieberson had picked fresh faces and fresh voices to sing most of the sparkling Rodgers and Hart songs—today's voices singing yesterday's music, and how well they meshed, how magnificent was the lush young voice of Shirley Verrett!

And after it was all over, a tall, bald man in the audience spoke for many when he murmured quietly, "There was our youth."

There may be times when the Music Theater will take an intermission, but certainly this is one part of Lincoln Center that will again and again come alive.

MARTHA SWOPE   1

2   MARTHA SWOPE

The *New York City Ballet*

(1) *Serenade;* (2) Melissa Hayden in *Trois Valses Romantiques;* and (3) Patricia McBride in *La Sonnambula.*

3   MARTHA SWOPE

MARTHA SWOPE 1

MARTHA SWOPE 2

(1) George Balanchine (*center*) and Lincoln Kirstein, Directors of the New York City Ballet, talking with a dancer.

(2) Marnee Morris (*in leotard*) and Renee Estopinal backstage.

(3) Balanchine (*center*) studies costume sketches for his ballet *Don Quixote* with Esteban Frances, who designed the costumes, set and scenic effects, and Mme. Barbara Karinska, costumer for the New York City Ballet.

(4) Balanchine directs a rehearsal.

3
4

MARTHA SWOPE   **1**

2

(1) Edward Villella in *Prodigal Son*, with Karen
von Aroldingen, and (2) Arthur Mitchell in *Four
Temperaments*.

1

2

(1) *Swan Lake,* with Patricia McBride and Edward Villella, and (2) *Stars and Stripes,* with Melissa Hayden and Jacques d'Amboise.

(3) Jacques d'Amboise, and (4) the corps de ballet in *The Nutcracker.*

3

4

The *New York City Opera*

(1) Beverly Sills and Michele Molese in *Manon,*
and (2) Norman Treigle in *Faust.*

1

2   3

(1) Julius Rudel, Director of the New York City Opera.

(2) Anne Elgar (*seated*) and Brenda Lewis in *Lizzie Borden*, and

(3) chorus members in *Soeur Angelica*.

(4) *Carry Nation*, with Beverly Wolff (*center*) as Carry and chorus members (*left to right*) Pearl Goldsmith, Donna Owens, and Marilyn Armstrong.

(5) At a rehearsal of *Roberto Devereux*, director Tito Capobianco (*center*) works with Beverly Wolff as Sarah and Placido Domingo as Roberto.

4

5

BETH BERGMAN

BETH BERGMAN

(1) Young performer Christopher Lee is rehearsed by director Frank Corsaro for his role in *Madame Butterfly*.

(2) Norman Treigle and Beverly Sills rehearse *Julius Caesar*.

(3) Salvador Novoa as the Duke of Bomarzo in Alberto Ginastera's *Bomarzo*.

(4) On March 29, 1961, construction workers erected a sign marking the site of the New York State Theater.

3

4

BOB SERATING

(1) On October 22, 1962, William Schuman (*right*) announced the appointment of Richard Rodgers as President and Producing Director of the New York Music Theater for the presentation of contemporary musicals at the New York State Theater.

(2) Richard Rodgers at the piano rehearses Florence Henderson and Giorgio Tozzi for their roles in the Music Theater's production of *South Pacific*, and on-stage (3) are Irene Byatt as Bloody Mary and David Doyle as Luther Billis in *South Pacific*.

(4) Rehearsing for the Music Theater's production of *West Side Story* are Barbara Luna, Victoria Mallory, Alan Castner, and Kurt Peterson.

2

3   FRIEDMAN-ABELES

FRIEDMAN-ABELES

4

FRIEDMAN-ABELES

(1) "Numbers, 1964" a 9 by 14 foot sculpmetal by Jasper Johns in the outer lobby of the New York State Theater.

(2) Richard M. Clurman, Chairman of the Board of City Center of Music and Drama, Inc., and member of the Board of Lincoln Center.

(3) Opening night of the New York State Theater, April 23, 1964.

(4) The New York State Theater.

BOB SERATING

GUY GILLETTE

1

2

COURTESY OF TIME INC.   3   GUY GILLETTE

4

the repertory
theater

"...We have the Metropolitan Opera Company next to us, the Philharmonic, the New York State Theater. Besides this, we are within a stone's throw of Broadway which exercises the ingenuity of the finest commercial theater in the world. Finally, we are being designated —potentially—as the National Theater of America. ...We are here to attempt to succeed, and to do so now...."
—Jules Irving, Director of the Repertory Theater of Lincoln Center

It seemed almost unfair. Every other constituent arrived at Lincoln Center at the peak of its reputation. Only the Repertory Theater was still in the seedling stage. Conceived with great expectations, born into controversy, it faced a future that demanded instant success.

Tradition takes time to develop. Trying to start the groundwork for such a tradition, Jules Irving said, "is like inventing your own fore-fathers." Even those critics friendliest to repertory theater admit that the American public is not accustomed to the idea of a permanent company performing several different plays in a single season. And it is difficult to build an audience that has a multiplicity of taste.

Indeed there are those who ask: Is this kind of theater really necessary?

Putting it plainly, one critic commented: "I don't think you need a repertory theater in New York. You've usually got a couple dozen shows on Broadway, and you can see one play tonight and another play tomorrow. As for the old plays— what entertained the Elizabethans who didn't have TV or radio or anything—those old plays aren't suitable now. I don't think most people want to spend ten dollars to see an antiquated bit of nonsense. Now if you're in San Diego or Savannah, where there are regional theaters, and you see amateurs fooling around on stage in some old nonsense, you'll put up with it, because you don't have any other theater. But when you're in New York, you've got all these new plays to pick from—and they can't be turkeys, they've got to be

good to survive. So you don't need repertory in New York."

But repertory theater doesn't have to mean an "antiquated bit of nonsense." Moreover because of the millions of people in New York City and the steady flow of tourists, there was good reason to hope for the existence of an aware, literate public willing to say of a repertory play, "Well, it's worth seeing because we might never see it anywhere else."

In its brief life the Repertory Theater has presented to its public a succession of plays drawn from both the classic and contemporary: Brecht, Molière, Shaw, Shakespeare, Wycherley, Jonson, Sartre and Lorca. In its ambitious opening season, it produced Buechner's *Danton's Death*, Wycherley's *The Country Wife*, the American premiere of Sartre's *The Condemned of Altona* and the New York premiere of Brecht's *Caucasian Chalk Circle*—the first time Brecht was success-fully produced in New York City.

But the growth of this kind of appreciative audience is a gradual process.

Repertory has a heritage in Europe where it is generally divided into two categories. There is the permanent trust fund of important plays that are usually presented in the styles appropriate to them by such prestigious groups as the National Theater in England, the Schiller Theater in West Berlin, the Royal Dramatic Theater in Stockholm. There is also the type of repertory founded by a great director or playwright with a personal quest, a particular style: Bertolt Brecht's Berliner Ensemble, Joan Littlewood's Theater Workshop in London, Stanislavski's Moscow Art Theater.

When the original Lincoln Center idea was created in the mid-1950's, there was no outstanding repertory company in America. We had only fledglings in the field, primarily regional: the Alley Theater in Houston, the Arena Stage in Washington, D.C., and the San Francisco Actor's Workshop.

The Lincoln Center Board sought out the experts. Most of the advisors were in general agreement on some negative proposals: Leave the Broadway musicals to Broadway; leave to Off-Broadway the uncharted areas of the offbeat; forget about the "cocktail school" of so-called

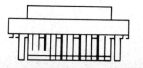

sophisticated drama. Repertory theater, in their view, also should not compete for that part of the general public who had deserted the theater for the movies fifty years ago and later left movies for television. If television was a supermarket, they said, repertory theater should be the gourmet shop.

"We cannot thrive only on what others have created for us in the past, any more than we can deprive ourselves of what our forbears from many lands have bequeathed," said critic Harold Clurman. "I believe, since we possess very few classics of our own, one of the main goals of an *American* repertory theater should be the development and production of native plays of serious intent and sound craftsmanship."

Taking into consideration these varied suggestions, the Lincoln Center Board decided to create its own Repertory Theater. To organize it the Board chose noted producer Robert Whitehead and the celebrated director Elia Kazan.

Kazan sounded the clarion, "We want a theater of themes, of relevance to the experience of living today. At Lincoln Center, we expect, on occasion to say, 'We're going to show you this play, whether you like it or not, simply because we believe it deserves your attention.' "

The Kazan-Whitehead plan put its emphasis on what they called "contemporary classics," plays of quality written in the past forty years. "These plays must be kept alive, and that means kept on stage. They describe the American experience and the contemporary condition. They are our theater heritage." But they also planned to do classics of other countries and other times. "The curse of the usual revival is that it brings nothing back to life at all. The play has not been reexperienced. It seems to us that there is no point in producing an old play unless the creative director has an idea for it that makes it necessary to be seen—when somehow, the director has reexperienced the play, and can make the audience reexperience it as well."

It sounded exciting. Lincoln Center provided $500,000 so that Whitehead and Kazan could start to select and train their acting troupe. Mrs. Vivian Beaumont Allen donated $3 million for a

house which was promptly designated the Vivian Beaumont Theater.

It was a venture with great flair and promise. Critic Kenneth Tynan noted that it could be "the most important thing ever done in the American theater."

The celebrated stage designer Jo Mielziner was among the experts called in for consultation by John D. Rockefeller 3rd. Mielziner expressed his view that most New York theaters were badly designed and were too large and that the theater's most urgent need was a greater sense of intimacy between audience and actor.

Intimacy was also the key word in the concept of Eero Saarinen, the brilliant and imaginative architect who would design the Beaumont Theater.

Working from the inside out, Saarinen and Mielziner made studies of precisely where the main stage action took place in more than 300 productions. Then, having charted the range of people's heights, they were able to determine the variations in eye-levels within a seated audience. They built full-sized mock-ups in an empty movie house in Pontiac, Michigan.

Out of this thorough study evolved the Saarinen-Mielziner version of the "thrust stage," an extension of the permanent stage into the audience. Removing seats or adding platforms to the "thrust" area allows for a variety of arrangements to suit the needs of the play. Saarinen designed his stage so that it could extend twenty-eight feet into the auditorium, which meant the audience was almost wrapped around the stage as people "might bunch around the fire on a cold night." The challenge was that each member of the audience must be able to see the expression in the eyes of a face as small as Julie Harris'.

This new concept of theater sweeps away the old theater of simple illusion. Not only is the audience watching the actor, but he is also aware of the rest of the audience sharing the experience. Saarinen kept his seats set at a rake and carefully spaced, so that the farthest seat was no more than sixty-four feet from the stage. For the audience the sense of intimacy is profound.

Flexibility was another key element in designing the theater. Acoustical, air-conditioning and lighting elements were all incorporated into a ribbed ceiling, with the lights pre-angled to cover every square yard of the stage. Mielziner provided space behind the stage for rear projection as well as for scenery storage and also suggested additional space for a large rehearsal room that would include a stage. This evolved into the Forum Theater for more experimental productions—a scaled-down auditorium with minimal facilities and just 299 seats (as compared to more than 1,000 in the Beaumont).

Eero Saarinen died before the building was completed and John Dinkaloo supervised the final construction. But Saarinen had created the intricate and delicately balanced design, including a sparkling lobby whose glass wall looks out onto a reflecting pool in a small, separate plaza.

Resting in the pool is the famous Henry Moore sculpture, "Reclining Figure." The idea for the monumental form actually came from "a little piece of bone I found in the garden," explained the British sculptor. Out of that evolved a magnificent work seventeen feet high, twenty-five feet long. Its actual installation in the pool was a rather traumatic event. Since trucks and cranes were not permitted in the plaza, the twenty-five-ton form had to be moved on rollers. And since there was yet no water in the pool and no base for the sculpture, it was a delicate process of moving it slightly this way and somewhat that way until it was finally where Moore thought it should be. After a surveyor made exact measurements, it was photographed from all angles to make sure it would be returned to precisely the same site at precisely the same level. The sculpture was then removed from the pool so that its base could be built.

The Repertory itself had run into a difficult problem. Their production schedule was based on the projected completion of the Beaumont in 1964, but it became clear that the building would be delayed a year. Kazan and Whitehead, however, wouldn't wait. They decided to erect a temporary theater on a site near Washington Square provided by New York University. When the Lincoln Center Board balked, Kazan and Whitehead got construction funds from the American National Theater and Academy, and the theater opened in January, 1964, with Arthur Miller's new play, *After the Fall*. It was Miller's first play in seven years with an all-star cast featuring Jason Robards, Jr., Barbara Loden, Faye Dunaway, David Wayne and Joseph Wiseman. Much of the rest of the cast formed the core of the company for the next two seasons, and Wiseman returned to star in *Oppenheimer*. But the following autumn subscribers dropped from 46,000 to 29,000. A second series of plays was offered, starting with a revival of *The Changeling* by Thomas Middleton and William Rowley. It was the first time Kazan had directed a classic, and it was both a critical and financial disaster. The other plays were much more successful, particularly Molière's *Tartuffe* and another play by Arthur Miller, *Incident at Vichy*.

George D. Woods, the Repertory's first President and then Chairman of the Board, and Robert L. Hoguet, Jr., the new President, were both unhappy with the Repertory's financial administration. They complained that they could not get facts and figures from Kazan and Whitehead; they couldn't even find out how much of a deficit was anticipated—something they had to know before fund-raising could be started. The feeling was that Kazan was a fine director and Whitehead a creative producer, but that money seemed to be slipping too easily past both of them.

Whitehead later countered, "If you want a great theater, you have to be ready to spend a great amount of money on it." And Kazan pointed out that repertory cannot be judged like the ordinary single-shot show—hit or flop. He noted that Laurence Olivier's repertory was the out-growth of a nine-year effort at Stratford and the Old Vic, that Olivier himself had said it takes about twenty-five years to build a real repertory company. Sir Tyrone Guthrie echoed the idea that creating a repertory theater was a fight for time, five years being the very minimum required. "And the first steps towards creating such a company had better not be taken in the full glare

of publicity—and the full blast of criticism—professional and amateur, mostly ignorant and hostile—that beats upon Lincoln Center."

"It seems to me an absolute cultural necessity for the American theater," Guthrie continued, "to have at least one theatrical 'institution' and company, not just to make money for investors, nor to make 'names' of the chief performers, but rather as a public service, like an art gallery, a library, or a symphony orchestra. It must be taken as axiomatic that such a company will not make any money, and may very probably lose a great deal."

Whitehead described that autumn of 1964 as a time of "rage, sorrow and frustration."

The fact was that President of Lincoln Center William Schuman had received a letter of resignation from Elia Kazan. He had held it quietly, without comment. And when Woods and Hoguet raised the question of a new administrator for the Repertory, Schuman suggested Herman Krawitz, Assistant Manager of the Metropolitan Opera, to replace Whitehead. Woods, Hoguet and Charles Spofford, then Chairman of the Executive Committee, all agreed. John D. Rockefeller 3rd, however, suggested that any such change must be made through the front door—that Schuman should discuss it with Anthony A. Bliss, President of the Met. Bliss was not happy about losing Krawitz to the Repertory, so Schuman passed the ball back to Hoguet for continued discussion.

In the meanwhile Schuman explored Krawitz's interest in the matter. "It was a very attractive offer, but there were many problems involved," said Krawitz. "I immediately discussed it with Mr. Bing. And I kept him posted on the situation at all times."

After prolonged negotiations, Krawitz finally refused the offer, reconsidered a more tempting offer and then refused that, too—always in consultation with Mr. Bing.

But then the brouhaha broke. Mr. Schuman had not made two important phone calls. He had not called Mr. Bing—presuming that Mr. Bliss would do this, and he had not called Mr. Whitehead, which somebody else was supposed to have done and had not.

Whitehead promptly resigned, saying he didn't want his job being bandied about in the market-

place without his knowing of it. The situation received widespread attention in all the news media. When Bing exploded in print that Schuman was trying to raid the Met, Schuman frankly admitted, "I should have called Bing."

Kazan also publicly resigned, although he had done so privately months before.

Schuman maintained a dignified silence, which did not help him with the general press and public. But at the next Lincoln Center Board meeting he was given a standing ovation.

For the struggling Repertory, the publicity was almost crushing. "Our theater will not spring to life, fully grown, in the middle of a building," wrote theater critic Robert Brustein in the *New Republic*. "If it is to be reborn, it must begin like an infant, taking its first tentative steps before very few interested observers; and only the shape of its growth will determine the shape of the building that grows around it."

The crossroads for the Repertory were crucial. Critics were excoriating the Repertory's Board members with complaints about bankers' interference in the Arts. The new Board President, Robert L. Hoguet, was deeply distressed about the next direction to take. Hoguet is a man of energy and enthusiasm, with little background in the theater but a strong record in management and administration as Executive Vice President of the First National Bank. His wife had been particularly active in Lincoln Center's early fund-raising days, and he had been drawn into its orbit. It was John D. Rockefeller 3rd and Charles Spofford who had persuaded him to accept the presidency of the Repertory Board. Then came Hoguet's search for new directors.

"I was sitting in a barber shop somewhere, reading the *Saturday Review*, when I saw a review of a show done in San Francisco by two fellows named Jules Irving and Herbert Blau," Hoguet remembered. "Subsequently, Michael Burke, who is on the Board, and I went to San Francisco, saw some of their productions, talked to them at length and then one morning shook hands in agreement at Trader Vic's Restaurant. And that was it."

The two new directors of the Repertory Theater were New Yorkers who had started the San Francisco Actor's Workshop from scratch and had achieved a national reputation after a dozen years. Irving and Blau not only operated two theaters, year round, in downtown San Francisco, but they had inaugurated a touring program for their actors throughout the California secondary schools. Furthermore, the State Department had picked their workshop to represent the United States at the Brussels World Fair in 1958. Despite the widespread fame of the new men, a large portion of the New York theater group had supported Whitehead and Kazan in the imbroglio, and automatically resented their replacements. But the reputation of Irving's and Blau's achievement on the Coast was such that they were grudgingly granted a moratorium on criticism—to allow the group to see what their new directors could do.

As far as the theatrical world knew, Blau was the visionary and the voice, and Irving the more practical man who placed himself quietly behind the scenes. But those who really knew them realized that the men shared many of each other's attributes. They also shared the same concept of theater, but Blau often acted as spokesman, and attracted national attention through his book *The Impossible Theater.*

Blau and Irving brought with them from San Francisco a few of their key people. One of them, Robert Symonds, was both an outstanding actor and director who would have a similar role at Lincoln Center.

"We started from scratch," Symonds noted. "All that was here was the building. In fact when we got here, that wasn't even finished yet. Even into our opening production of *Danton's Death,* there was still a great deal of construction going on. But compared to what we had in San Francisco, everything here was lush. The one thing, of course, was that we had moved into a very, very hot spotlight."

One of Symonds' jobs was to help find the right plays to produce. "The Beaumont was designed to destroy the box set," he said. "Well, that's fine, except that so many dramas are written with that set in mind. The thrust stage is great for Greek drama, but it's tough on Restoration comedy. That type of comedy calls for a lot of people coming in and out of a lot of doors, and a thrust stage has no doors."

After the problems of opening plays, there's always the problem of finding audiences for them. The audience for repertory is generally one that cares enough about "Theater" to be interested in all kinds of plays, old and new, classic and experimental. And as Aline McMahon, one of Lincoln Center Repertory's major players, has pointed out, perhaps the ultimate realization of repertory is in an audience who has grown to care about the company, so that they will come back again and again just to see what the actors can do with different roles. The development of such an audience in a city unaccustomed to repertory theater is a slow, educational process.

The repertory audience is special, but the repertory troupe must also be special. Every repertory company maintains a permanent core of people on year-round salary. The luxury of this is that the play in production may have, for example, only a few parts for women, but the rest of the actresses will still be on salary, even though they are not working.

"The British National Theater can do that, [they have a company of 75 members] because they're subsidized by the British government," emphasized Alan Mandell, General Manager of Lincoln Center's Repertory Theater. "But we don't have the money to do it on that scale. If we did have such a permanent company, we could then say to any actor, 'You're going to play this role,' and there would be no discussion about it. They would do it. Under our system, we have to find the actors we want and then ask them if they would be willing to play the parts we want them to play. There are a great many Broadway stars who can't stand the long runs. After three or four months in one play, they feel they get stale. What we can offer is a limited engagement of no more than eight weeks. We can say, 'Come in and do this! Do it for kicks! You won't make a great deal of money but it's the role you've always wanted to do. Come and do it!' And many of them do."

When Irving and Blau arrived at Lincoln Center, they found a large number of actors and actresses under long-term contract. Since they needed to create their own company and had brought with them some of their own people, the weeding out and the blending was a sensitive task.

Some of the actors, of course, asked to break their contract.

It was Robert Whitehead who, long after he had left Lincoln Center, warned, "The Beaumont wasn't built to be a subsidized extension of Broadway, but the home of a great acting company. That object mustn't be relinquished too quickly."

One difficulty that Blau and Irving encountered was that American actors have received their basic training on the proscenium stage, and most have developed a subjective approach to acting. The open thrust stage at the Beaumont demands a different kind of performance, a certain grandeur of style.

"Out on the thrust stage, like ours," explained Jules Irving, "an actor is in a sense naked, fully exposed to the world. He has to have security and nobility of presence. Some actors are somewhat at a loss when pushed forward onto the open stage. I imagine that their predicament may be rather like that of the first Greek actors who found themselves having to address an audience of 6,000 in the arena. So what must be developed for our kind of stage are actors who have authority, magnitude, stature."

Aline McMahon has all those things. Besides her obvious talent, she has a deep understanding of her craft. "In a curious way," she notes, "the thrust stage persuades you to enlarge the scope of the part. The proscenium stage persuades you to encompass it, to shrink it, to bring it down finer and finer and finer. I don't know why that is, but I think it has to do with the fact that there's a roof over your head and a hundred lights around the edges of a proscenium stage. No matter how big that proscenium stage is, you're very limited in space, and you're tight, and you learn to pull in. But on the thrust stage, you feel you're playing in an enormous amphitheater. I think it has to do with the dark air above the actor's heads. The lights are out and you do not see the audience. Even though the audience is very close to you, the actor feels no intimacy at all."

Miss McMahon, however, was delighted with everything about the Repertory Theater—from the facilities to the close working relationships. "You get to know one another well. You make allowances and adjustments and you learn to count on certain qualities in certain actors. Repertory has no drawbacks for the actor. If you're young, the more you play, the better. And if you're getting older, as I am, it's wonderful to play a variety of parts."

Frederick Brahms is casting director at Lincoln Center Repertory. "There are any number of ways that any single role can be played," Brahms said. "For example, in *Saint Joan*, the Dauphin has been played as a gibbering idiot, and he's also been played as a very sly guy. The director tells me how he sees the Dauphin, and his concept greatly influences the sort of actor I would bring in to read for him."

Ray Fry, for example, had a small role in *King Lear*, then a good-sized part in *A Cry of Players* and a larger one in a play at the Forum. He was even alternating in two plays at the same time. "Repertory gives an actor the ability to stretch his talent," he commented.

Repertory offered Lee J. Cobb a chance to fulfill a lifetime wish to play King Lear. His acceptance of the role meant considerable financial sacrifice for him, but it also meant great personal satisfaction. "With the Lincoln Center Repertory Theater the conditions are as good as they can be. I don't have to play every night . . . and there is time to grow with each performance." Cobb added that he would be similarly delighted to return to repertory to do a low comedy or a musical "if it's distinctive enough."

Faced with the practicality of minimal budgets and no government subsidy, Jules Irving developed a realistic vision of the Repertory's future. He planned to keep the permanent company a small core of players who could be easily alternated in smaller roles. For some of the star parts, he hoped to attract other talented performers who might ultimately regard Lincoln Center Repertory as a kind of home base. "They play with us when there are roles they're interested in playing that we want them to play. When there's nothing for them with us, then they can go off and do whatever else they want. They may just do one play a season, or they may do all four in any one season, or they may skip a couple seasons, but our Repertory would be their focal point, and they would be identified with us.''

To attract such performers, the Repertory must achieve a pattern of success. When *Galileo* received excellent notices, the casting director got a stream of solicitations from agents of well-known actors saying, ''Keep so-and-so in mind. He would like to appear with you.''

Irving hopes to attract playwrights in the same way. But repertory does not offer the playwright the advantage it offers the actor. If a writer's play fails on Broadway, it might still be produced elsewhere; but if his play fails in repertory first, it fails with finality. Broadway producers simply do not wish to invest in a new production of a repertory failure.

However there are all kinds of plays that seem too noncommercial for Broadway. Yet if they're done successfully in repertory, they can have a prolonged life. *Summertree*, which originated at the Forum Theater, was later revived Off-Broadway. *In the Matter of J. Robert Oppenheimer* was originally under option to Robert Whitehead for Broadway production. But it seemed to require too large a budget for commercial success, so he released it for nonprofit production in Los Angeles. Jules Irving then brought it to the Beaumont and later prepared it for a national tour. Repertory can actually do for a playwright what it did for Chekhov. *The Seagull* was a commercial fiasco, but the Moscow Art Theater incorporated it into its repertoire. It was there that with the passage of time, this now classic play achieved commercial success.

A more immediate inducement for new playwrights at the Repertory Theater of Lincoln Center is the small Forum Theater.

The Forum is a simple amphitheater surrounded by black-curtained walls, carpeted in red and filled with dark brown seats. It has a black thrust stage with exposed lights overhead. ''There's a certain rawness in the theater that I like,'' noted Jules Irving. ''It's a theater that belongs to the play and the actors. This is where we try out exciting new scripts, devoid of commercial pressures and introduce actors who may join the company. We can also do established plays that require such a setting.''

The Forum opened with two one-act plays by Mayo Simon: *Walking to Waldheim* and *Happiness.* Simon was delighted with the production, and so were some of the critics. Even more successful was the subsequent production of 22-year-old Ron Cowan's *Summertree,* which won unanimous critical acclaim, and even made some money. But the financial support for the Forum has come from a Rockefeller Foundation grant and from the $100,000 supplied by the Federal Government via the National Arts Endowments Committee. Roger L. Stevens, the former Chairman of that committee, and a well-known theater producer himself, stated simply, ''Experimental professional theater is an essential part of the American theater.''

To find plays for the Beaumont and the Forum to produce, Repertory readers go through thousands of scripts, seek out the promising playwrights, coax them into any rewrites needed, then make the final selection.

The problems of any single play are not necessarily typical but they may serve as illustration. *Galileo*, for example, was selected for production at the Beaumont. Everything seemed smooth when both the director and leading players were chosen. But the director resigned, and the star became sick and asked to be excused. Then the search was on: Who did they think could play Galileo well, and who would be a good director? They wanted John Hirsch to direct, but he was at Stratford, Ontario, directing Shakespearean plays; his agent agreed that Hirsch might get free to do *Galileo,* but he first wanted to know whom they had cast for the lead.

There were several Americans who would have been good in the lead role, but none of them was available at the time. And Actor's Equity was reluctant to consent to Anthony Quayle because he was not an American performer. After considerable discussion, however, Quayle got his clearance.

General Manager Alan Mandell, another member of the original Blau-Irving group in San Francisco, then had to discuss budget with

the stage designer. Mandell described his role this way: "I'm not here just to keep the deficit down. I'm here to see that everything that can be done will be done to get good theater on that stage. I'm not against making money, but the most important thing is what happens on stage. I know that."

Mandell is the kind of General Manager who not only handles delicate labor negotiations but even performs on stage, learning an entire role overnight when necessary.

"That's why I know that you just can't make business decisions in the theater the way you can at General Motors," he said. "For example, here we had a new director on *Galileo*, and he had his own ideas about the stage design. Now the scenic designer had worked with the previous director, and he had to throw a lot of his earlier work out of the window. The same was true of the man who did the costumes. This meant a readjusted budget, spending more money than we figured. At one point, the designer came to me and said, 'Unless I have the Pope's coat made in this particular way, it will ruin the effect of this scene.' Well, I had watched rehearsals, and it was clear to me that what he had designed in that particular scene did depend a great deal on the full effect of the way the Pope walked out, and the design of his coat *was* that important. Well, maybe that wasn't an obvious business decision, but it was a necessary decision for the best theater."

Rather than have special music composed for *Galileo*, Mandell took on the job of tracking down the original score in Germany. Finally tracing it to its source, he then had to negotiate royalties with the agent. There was also a decision on whether to use taped music or a small, live orchestra, as well as a search for singers, including two small boys. Mandell heard that *The Magic Flute* was being done at the Metropolitan, so he got the phone numbers of two boy singers in it and hired them. "Suddenly, I had the feeling that I was raiding the Met," Mandell said, smiling.

The State Theater made available extra rehearsal rooms for *Galileo*, Philharmonic Hall hired *Galileo's* "extras" as ushers and the

director of the five-piece orchestra for *Galileo* doubled as rehearsal pianist for the New York City Opera.

The play opened to critical praise. "It played to 99 percent of capacity," explained Jeanette Sponik, who operates the Repertory Business Office, "yet we had to close it before we wanted to, because we had a commitment to rent our theater for the Summer Festival." An advantage of Repertory, however, is that the play, and its props and sets, are available for use in the future.

The outdoor posters for *Galileo*, like all the other Repertory Theater posters, were done by art students at Prátt Institute. Initiating and supervising this graphics program was Susan Bloch, who also handles publicity, advertising and a dozen other duties. A part-time artist and serious student of art, Miss Bloch not only understood the value of giving public recognition to talented students, but also saw the graphics program as still another way to save money for the Repertory. Everybody at Repertory is earnestly cost-conscious.

The maintenance cost of the Repertory Theater comes close to $500,000 a year. This includes the Repertory's share toward the central air conditioning, heating plant and security guards for the whole of Lincoln Center.

"One of the ways we might cut costs," said Miss Sponik, "is the idea of a central box office for the entire Lincoln Center. I don't know if it's feasible, but it's worth considering. As it is, all the subscription departments of all the constituents here do cooperate whenever we can. For example, we all swap lists."

Robert Schlosser supervises the subscription system at the Repertory Theater, just as he did in the San Francisco Actor's Workshop. When he arrived here he found the subscription department to be so automated that seat requests were fed into a computer. But the computer was still not sophisticated enough to handle all the variables—such as the woman who wanted a certain seat because she was deaf in one ear, or the man with a stiff knee who needed a left aisle seat. "You have no idea of the number of different combinations you can receive," Schlosser said. "The computers we can afford just can't cope with all those combinations. Besides, when a subscriber calls and complains about a seat, you can't plug the phone into a computer."

The complications became ominous when the computer missed an entire box of orders, representing 1,000 subscriptions. The automated system was scrapped in favor of human beings.

Repertory depends on subscription sales to furnish some of its financial backbone for future productions. Now even the experimental Forum Theater has had to go on a subscription basis. Subscribers at both theaters, however, are offered the privilege of exchanging tickets for other dates, something not usually done in subscription series.

The business end of Lincoln Center Repertory is of more critical concern than it might be in the commercial theater. A Broadway producer bets on a hit and the gamble is great—but if he makes it, the box office pays the bills. Lincoln Center Repertory has no such financial hopes, because every play only has a limited engagement. One of the rare exceptions was *In the Matter of J. Robert Oppenheimer* by Heinar Kipphardt, which was extended through the summer in 1969. Staged by Jules Irving, *Oppenheimer* was also the first national touring production of the Repertory Theater. Gordon Davidson, artistic director of the Mark Taper Forum in Los Angeles and director of the Beaumont production for Lincoln Center, commented ruefully, "Believe me, ever since I've been in what we call 'institutional theater' I've talked and thought more about money than I ever did when I was in the commercial theater."

Robert L. Hoguet, who became Chairman of the Board of Lincoln Center Repertory, explained, "If a show costs three dollars to put on, you get two dollars from the ticket sale and you have to go to the public for the other dollar. That dollar comes more easily to the opera or the symphony or the ballet because the public has been used to the idea of contributing to them, but they just aren't used to the idea yet of giving money to theater."

To help convince the public, the Repertory drafted former actor-director Robert Montgomery as its new President. Montgomery has since

resigned, but he was always aware of the basic problems.

"Larry Olivier's financial problems are solved at one shot, with three people," Montgomery remarked enviously. "He sits down with a member of the National Arts Council and a member of the London Arts Council—they both hand him a check and he goes away! When he told me about this, I said, 'Larry, you are asking me to take out British citizenship.' "

Both Hoguet and Montgomery feel that if Theater is to survive, government subsidy is inevitable. In the meanwhile, Montgomery sees hope in exploring money-saving possibilities on a Center-wide basis. Pointing to one example, Montgomery said, "Suppose, just *suppose,* it were possible to build all the scenery in one place for all the constituents in Lincoln Center, and have a twelve-month operation going on in the Scenery Department."

But the questions of costs only have meaning when balanced with the quality of play selection and production. Soon after Herbert Blau resigned in 1968, Jules Irving got a new contract which gave him complete control of play selection and casting. To help subscription sales Irving invited Mike Nichols to direct a special all-star production of Lillian Hellman's, *The Little Foxes.* He began to put an increased emphasis on American plays which brought great attention to the Repertory Theater as our country's "national theater."

"Jules is one in a million, a fellow who knows the whole literature," Robert Hoguet emphasized. "He not only knows how to recognize great creativity in other people, but he's an extraordinary organizer, a tough, hard-boiled guy who can read a balance sheet just as well as the vice-president of a bank."

Irving needs all those qualities. The British National Theater, fully subsidized, can blithely satisfy its preference for a first-rate work that will play to less than capacity, rather than a third-rate one that may fill the house. But Irving must somehow balance his selections to maintain both the quality and the budget. Nobody judges the success of a symphony by the number of people who have heard it or the worth of a

painting by the number of people who have seen it. As Gordon Davidson, the director of *Oppenheimer*, put it: "The trouble is that the theater is equated with show business, which is judged by financial success."

Clive Barnes of *The New York Times* has called the Lincoln Center Repertory Theater "the best repertory company in the country." As for the Forum Theater, even when he was critical of individual plays there, Barnes pointed out that the theater was doing exactly what it should be doing—giving excellent productions of experimental works and presenting promising playwrights to the public. "The most important aspect of the Forum Theater," Barnes wrote, "is that it offers the company the total, essential right to fail."

Beyond the development of the Lincoln Center Repertory Theater, Jules Irving hopes for the day when the American public will accept theater as an integral part of their culture, as they now accept music. And as a corollary to that he would like to see more of a marriage of all the talent at Lincoln Center.

"One of my dreams when I first came here," he said, "was that one day there might be an event at Lincoln Center in which somebody from my theater would direct the production, Balanchine do the choreography, Bernstein write the music, and the performers would come from all the constituents."

Critic Richard Craven once said, "In the theater, you can't make a living—you can only make a fortune."

Through its struggle for existence, the Lincoln Center Repertory Theater may still, one day, reap its fortune.

(1) Jules Irving, Director of the Repertory Theater, takes time from his many other responsibilities to work with Wardrobe Head Mariana Torres (*left*) and Costume Designer Carrie Fishbein Robbins as the final touches are put on the make-up of actor Michael Dunn, who appeared in William Hanley's *The Inner Journey*.

(2) Designer Jo Mielziner (*left*), playwright Arthur Miller (*center*), and producer-director Elia Kazan discuss the Repertory Theater's first production, the premiere of Mr. Miller's *After the Fall*.

(3) The Vivian Beaumont Theater, home of the Repertory Theater of Lincoln Center, with the reflecting pool and Henry Moore's bronze sculpture "Lincoln Center Reclining Figure" in the foreground.

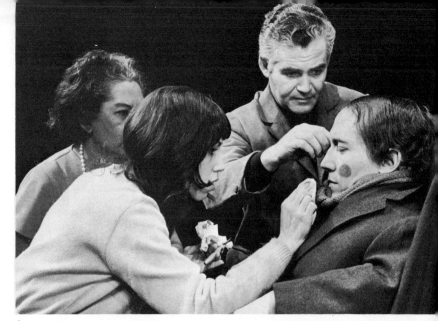

1   MARTHA SWOPE

2   MARTHA SWOPE
3   EZRA STOLLER © ESTO

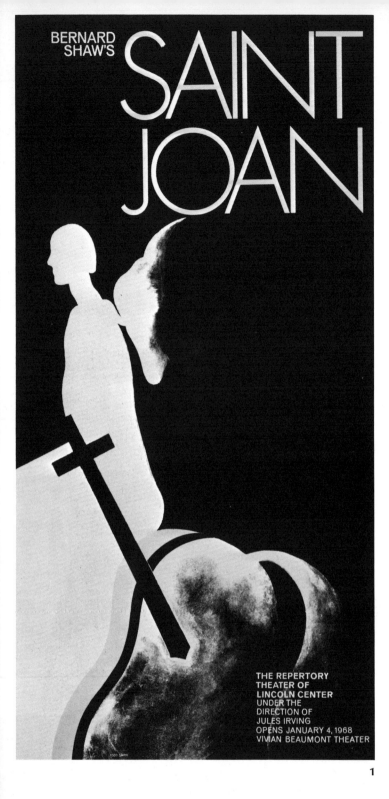

BERNARD
SHAW'S
SAINT
JOAN

THE REPERTORY
THEATER OF
LINCOLN CENTER
UNDER THE
DIRECTION OF
JULES IRVING
OPENS JANUARY 4, 1968
VIVIAN BEAUMONT THEATER

1

THE REPERTORY
THEATER OF
LINCOLN CENTER
UNDER THE
DIRECTION OF
JULES IRVING

EDMOND ROSTAND'S
CYRANO
DE BERGERAC

IN A NEW ENGLISH VERSION BY JAMES FORSYTH

OPENS APRIL 25, 1968
VIVIAN BEAUMONT THEATER

2

Some of the posters for productions of the Repertory
Theater are designed by students at Pratt Institute.
The artists, in order of their posters' appearance are,
(1) Todd Smith, (2) David Palladini, (3) Edward Krent,
(4) Brian Kelly.

BERTOLT BRECHT'S "GALILEO" / ENGLISH VERSION BY CHARLES LAUGHTON
OPENS APRIL 13, 1967 / VIVIAN BEAUMONT THEATER
THE REPERTORY THEATER OF LINCOLN CENTER

under the
direction of
JULES IRVING

3

OPENS OCTOBER 26, 1967   **THE REPERTORY**
VIVIAN BEAUMONT THEATER   **THEATER OF**
LINCOLN CENTER
JULES IRVING,
DIRECTOR
PRESENTS

LILLIAN
HELLMAN'S   **THE
LITTLE
FOXES**

BRIAN KELLY

4

MARTHA SWOPE   1

MARTHA SWOPE   2

(1) Diana Sands as Joan of Arc in Bernard Shaw's *Saint Joan*.

(2) Robert Symonds as Harpagon in Molière's *The Miser*.

(3) *Cyrano de Bergerac* by Edmond Rostand, with Robert Symonds (*far left*) as Cyrano.

(4) *The Country Wife* by William Wycherley, with Ray Fry (*left*) as Sir Jasper Fidget, Priscilla Pointer as My Lady Fidget, and Stacy Keach as Mr. Horner.

3

4

MARTHA SWOPE   **1**

(1) Lillian Hellman's *The Little Foxes* with George C. Scott and Margaret Leighton (*foreground*), Anne Bancroft and E. G. Marshall (*seated*), and William Prince and Austin Pendleton (*standing*).

(2) *In the Matter of J. Robert Oppenheimer* by Heinar Kipphardt, with Joseph Wiseman (*foreground*) as Oppenheimer and (*left to right*) Eduard Franz, Harry Townes, and Whitfield Connor.

(3) The American premiere of Harold Pinter's *Landscape* and *Silence* was presented by the Repertory in the Forum Theater of the Vivian Beaumont Theater. Shown here are Robert Symonds and Mildred Natwick in *Landscape*.

MARTHA SWOPE   **2**

(1) *Galileo* by Bertolt Brecht.

(2) Shakespeare's *King Lear* with Lee J. Cobb (*right*) as Lear, Robert Stattel (*left*) as Edgar, and Stephen Elliott as Gloucester.

(3) Jean Giraudoux's *Tiger at the Gates*, translated by Christopher Fry, with Philip Bosco (*center*) as Hector.

MARTHA SWOPE   1

MARTHA SWOPE   2

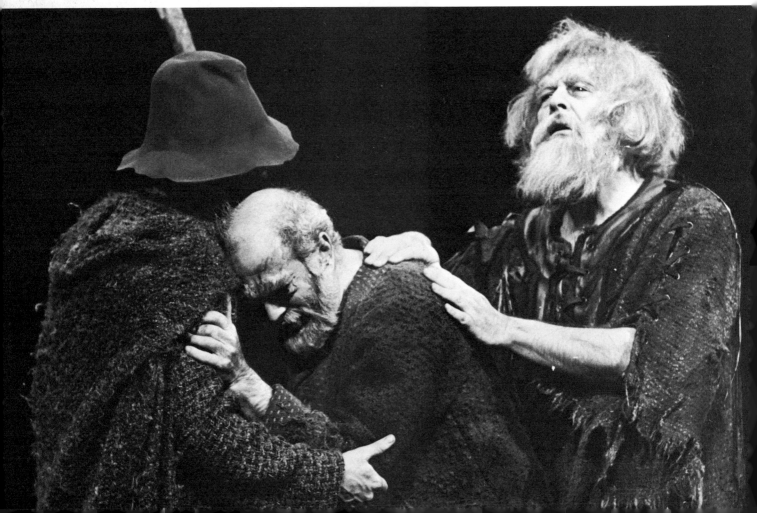

(1) Anne Bancroft and Jackie Paris in William Gibson's *A Cry of Players*.

(2) *The Year Boston Won the Pennant*, by John Ford Noonan, which was introduced in the Forum Theater, with Roy R. Scheider (*left*) and Paul Benjamin.

INGE MORATH, MAGNUM 1

MARTHA SWOPE 2

MARTHA SWOPE
WILLIAM F. THATCHER

3
4

(1) Arthur Miller's *After the Fall*, with Jason Robards, Jr., and Barbara Loden.

(2) William Saroyan's *The Time of Your Life* with (*left to right*) Susan Tyrrell, Biff McGuire, (*sitting*) James Broderick, Priscilla Pointer, (*background, on steps*) Robert Symonds, and Leonard Frey.

(3) Actor Judd Jones (*right*) with students after a Lincoln Center Student Program production of Martin Duberman's *In White America*.

(4) The Repertory Theater of Lincoln Center in Boston on its first national tour.

the library
& museum
of the
performing arts

> "If you give this idea importance, it can be the heart and justification of Lincoln Center—it can bring it all together."
> —Carleton Sprague Smith, 1957

"It is quite a chicken you hatched all those many years ago," wrote Lauder Greenway, one of the original members of the Lincoln Center Exploratory Committee, to Carleton Sprague Smith ten years later.

That chicken, the Library & Museum of the Performing Arts, seems tucked away in the corner of things, but it is not a quiet corner—there, in fact, is where much of the action is.

It's a mixed kind of action, and the Library & Museum of the Performing Arts often becomes the most exciting place in the plaza. The excitement can be sensed as soon as one sees Alexander Calder's striking stabile in front of the building. An abstract, open work of blackened steel, it is called "Le Guichet." It's a great peekaboo place for the children.

The expansive glass front of the building itself invites exploration of the Library & Museum. Inside, the impression of excitement is reinforced. The lighting and the carpeting and the corners and corridors combine to produce an anticipation of surprise.

The first surprise is easily found. Scattered about on the plaza floor, as well as on the floor above, are a number of stereophonic audio units that look like coffee tables. These audio drums, affectionately called "Asiels," are each equipped with a turntable and two sets of earphones and control buttons, and provide the finest in stereophonic sound. The soft, leather seats nearby are always occupied and the earphones are always warm—an elderly man listening to Bach and peacefully relaxing, a teenager grooving to Rock, and now and then singing aloud. Nobody says shh here. The "Asiels" are a memorial gift from the Nelson I. Asiel family in memory of their son and brother Robert who loved to listen to music. Thirty thousand records on open shelves are available to anybody for listening—and you don't even need a library card.

Up the wide stairway, past a spectacular mural of Shakespearean characters, is the Children's Library. In it is a charming jewel of a playhouse called "Heckscher Oval," where nearly a hundred children squeal delightedly at a puppet show. Downstairs in an intimate auditorium, some two hundred people are engrossed in a program of "Forgotten Songs," sung by talented young members of the Metropolitan Opera Studio. Elsewhere people of all ages wander through a walk-in exhibit of circus history, complete with clowns and gladiators, splashy posters two stories tall and a slide show of the thrills on mammoth screens. Still other people view a multiscreened, kaleidoscopic movie starring everyone from the Beatles to the Ballet Folklorico of Mexico to Leonard Bernstein. And in a single exhibit in the Main Gallery is the whole story of how an opera is created, designed, directed and performed.

And those are only a few of the changing attractions.

"Here's why it's unique," said John M. Cory, Deputy Director of The New York Public Library, which operates the Library & Museum: "If you go in expecting to find a library, you'd think it was the most interesting library you'd ever been in and wouldn't realize it was a museum. If you go in expecting to find a museum, you'd think it was an extremely interesting museum, and not realize you were in a library."

The idea of "museums of music" was originated in 1917 by Oscar Sonneck of the Library of Congress. And the man most responsible for developing the concept was Dr. Carleton Sprague Smith who at various times has been critic, author, musician, diplomat, linguist, teacher, Chief of the Music Division of The New York Public Library, and Board member of the New York Philharmonic and the Metropolitan Opera Association.

Dr. Smith first wrote about the possibility of museums of music in 1932, and Nelson Rockefeller put up money to help develop the idea. John D. Rockefeller 3rd activated the plan by making Smith a member of the Exploratory Committee of Lincoln Center for the Performing Arts.

Dr. Smith is persuasive: "We have hundreds of museums for the Arts, and we even have a

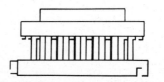

museum just for sculpture. But we didn't have a place where things come alive.

"Why shouldn't we bring recordings and performances to this silent library? And why should the scholar and specialist have to go to all the trouble of copying out a score, when a string quartet can be heard playing from the original parts? Music is a little bit like hieroglyphics—unless it's played, it doesn't mean anything. I went up to the Metropolitan Museum and there were all these musical instruments on display, and I was told, 'We regard this as furniture.' Well it shouldn't be. In the same way, costumes can come alive in a living fashion show. And why shouldn't you be able to see, in color the sets of *Don Giovanni,* used in 1795, or 1860, or any year? All that is really part and parcel of the performing arts."

Other advisors elaborated on the idea. Davidson Taylor, assisted by such experts as Howard Taubman of *The New York Times*—who had been advising on many aspects of the Center —developed a detailed report. The concept how-ever, was quietly compromised by budget. The original cost estimate for Lincoln Center had multiplied and there just wasn't enough money for everything. Finally it was decided to combine the Library & Museum with the Repertory Theater in a single building. But there was consid-erable doubt that such strong individualists as architects Eero Saarinen (for the Repertory) and Gordon Bunshaft of Skidmore, Owings & Merrill (for the Library) could unify their thinking on such a project.

"Right after Eero and I agreed to work together," Bunshaft recalled, "I got a rough idea of this umbrella thing. I called Eero on a Friday and sold it to him over the phone, and he thought it was wonderful. About three days later he came to New York with a model of it. From then on we worked really together, and the Library & Museum and the Beaumont became one element, interlocked. But together we were just concerned with the overall chassis—the concept, the materials, the dimensions—we never got involved with each other's interior aesthetics.

"We had one fight, a real hot one, about spacing the columns in front. He wanted a pair of columns in the corner, and I thought it was wrong. We were also debating about who would do the working drawings, and we were getting nowhere. Well, I came in one morning and I said, 'Eero, you let me have my way on those columns and you can do the working drawings,' and he was delighted. But Eero died before it was all done."

Unlike the architects of some of the other buildings, Bunshaft had few complications and made few compromises. "We had a wonderful client in The New York Public Library," he said. "They knew what they wanted to do in there. We tried to solve the function of it in terms of our times. Ours wasn't a great architectural problem, expressing the library. The library is a series of smaller elements. That's probably why having the library alone might not have produced a distinguished building—because there isn't any great single element in it. But with the mixture of the two, the library and the theater—and the umbrella of the top floor housing the Research Library and acting as a unifier for the structure of the thing—it worked out. Besides, we just couldn't put two buildings in that area. There wasn't room."

Since the concept of a combined library and museum was unique, it presented a budgeting problem for the City of New York and The New York Public Library. The cost of books and salaries fit in with normal City allocations for the Branch Library System, but what about the museum? It was the Library's Deputy Director John Cory who searched through the City Code to discover Section 492 entitled "Promotional and Celebrational Expenses," which provided for exhibits "to publicize a health or educational program." The flexible phrasing seemed to fit, and the City appropriated an initial $100,000. They cut this to zero in the next budget, then were persuaded to allot $25,000 yearly, mainly for maintenance.

The grant for a children's theater by the Heckscher Foundation was not only a gift of money, but a gift of imagination. The architect saw the theater as a room-within-a-room that would draw children toward it for a peek inside. "He thinks with his pencil," Cory commented admiringly of Bunshaft. "The Heckscher Oval was his impromptu contribution." The Oval is a self-contained playhouse within the Children's Library of the General Library. It has its own stage, movie projector and piano, and presents films, magic and puppet shows, pantomime, concerts, plays, readings and story-hours. "We almost can't advertise our upcoming programs, because we then get three times as many children as we have seats," observed Dr. Robert Henderson, Chief of the General Library and the Shelby Cullom Davis Museum of the Performing Arts. The feeling here is that the Heckscher Oval should be in constant use, with specially designed programs for different age groups at different hours. However the use of the Oval must be limited to Saturdays and to the occasional week-days when class tours from various schools are specifically scheduled. There are seats for sixty, but a hundred children can squeeze in when the chairs are removed—and there is often an overflow crowd. The films draw so many children that the downstairs auditorium must often be used. But keeping the Oval always open and busy—and there is no shortage of program ideas—requires more money and more staff, and neither is now on the horizon.

Outside the Oval are the small reading tables and the open shelves with 5,000 record albums and 13,000 books, mostly related to the perform-ing arts.

"Many of the records and books here are on a sophisticated level," noted Mary Strang, the Children's Librarian. "We don't offer simplified kiddy versions of masterpieces. Our recording of Shakespeare's *Hamlet* is the Gielgud performance. Our recording of Beethoven's Ninth is the complete symphony, not a potpourri of excerpts. Three 12-year-old boys came in one day asking if we had any of the Tijuana Brass records. We didn't have any, so we suggested that they try a Mozart horn concerto. They loved it, and they were here for hours playing different horn con-certos. That's the kind of thing we always hope will happen, and sometimes does."

Like the rest of Lincoln Center, the Children's Library is geared primarily to the performing arts. It therefore attracts many budding performers and children of Lincoln Center players as well as the neighborhood youngsters.

This area of the Library belongs to the children and caters to them. Children have little interest in an original Mozart letter or a mural depicting Elizabethan England or an exhibit of Irving Berlin's sheet music. But they're fascinated with a display of puppets and marionettes from China, India and Thailand—particularly since they are allowed to operate some of the puppets themselves. The exhibit cases are even fashioned with peep holes at various heights for children of various sizes. And if costumes or masks are being shown, the children are encouraged to try them on.

"I wish I could take all these things home," said one little boy.

"I wish this was my home," said a little girl.

For some the Vincent Astor Gallery is history; for others it's nostalgia. This gallery, a gift from Mrs. Vincent Astor, a trustee of The New York Public Library, is situated in its own alcove open-ing off the Main Gallery. It serves as a showcase for a variety of performing art treasures—from original costumes of old operas to the family letters of Mendelssohn to Oscar Wilde's hand-written manuscript for *The Importance of Being Earnest*; from Irene Castle's dancing shoes to the bonnet Katharine Cornell wore in *The Barretts of Wimpole Street*.

The mood changes downstairs. Below the main floor and facing Amsterdam Avenue, there is another world featuring original art, photography and design associated with the performing arts. The Amsterdam Gallery, like all the other galleries and exhibits, is the concern of Paul Seiz. His emphasis throughout the building is on "interpre-tative exhibitions," such as those showing the history of the circus and the step-by-step development of an opera.

"We wanted to show how a typical opera is put together," Seiz explained. "We chose *Die Frau ohne Schatten* by Richard Strauss and documented it from its very inception, from Strauss' first correspondence about the opera's idea. The Met was doing a new production of it

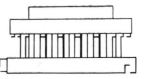

115

then, so we tape-recorded interviews with the designer and director, and used them in the exhibit. Then we documented the progress of the whole thing, from the construction of the sets to the actual performance, using color slides and recordings."

Among the other projects Seiz hopes to do are a similar exhibit of a single ballet; a behind-the-scenes story of television, complete with cameras, booms, lights and some buttons that will make things move—and with directors and actors explaining the action on a real set; and an audio-visual exhibit about the development of the orchestra, tracing it from its earliest history and relating it to the whole spectrum of society.

The central hum and throb of the Library & Museum is the auditorium—a small place with a bare stage, no facilities for scenery and staging, no dressing rooms. Dr. Robert Henderson, Chief of the General Library & Museum, talked about it with obvious warm affection.

"The marvel of that auditorium is that it's almost never empty, never quiet," he remarked wonderingly. "Whatever you want, you name it, we show it. Well, almost," he added smilingly.

"In a sample year," Henderson continued, "we have more than four hundred concerts and film showings. We also seem to serve as a show-case for the singers of the Metropolitan Opera Studio and some of the young soloists at the Philharmonic, and we've even had choreographers discussing and demonstrating the intricacies of the dance. Besides, we're always putting on short experimental theater productions that you wouldn't see anywhere else. And the beautiful part of it all is that admission is absolutely free.

"We have certain limitations," Henderson reflected, "but we try to ignore them."

While the auditorium promotes living music and lively theater, the General Library is still the heart of the place. It's a mixed-bag kind of library, because its collection, limited to the performing arts, contains almost an equal number of books and records, a total of 100,000, including 50,000 musical scores. Except for materials in the reference section, anything may be taken out by anyone with a library card. About 35,000 items

are circulated each month, and almost half of those are phonograph records.

"Some of our records take a beating, particularly the popular music," said Ralph Long, Coordinator of the General Library, "but the main thing is that our material is used and wanted. The availability of these records brings in a large proportion of young people."

The Library & Museum is physically divided into two separate parts: the General Library & Museum, which comprise the first four floors, and the Research Library, which occupies the fifth floor and spreads out—like an umbrella, as Gordon Bunshaft noted—over the top of the attached Repertory Theater. Chief of the Research Library is Thor Wood, a young man of manifest dedication.

The Research Library has the kind of quiet tone one would expect. Most of the people there are professionals, the working theater people and the serious students. This floor houses the Music Division (headed by Frank Campbell), which is the most heavily used collection of its kind in the United States and second in size only to that of the Library of Congress. It contains more than 200,000 volumes, with special strength in American music, including folk songs. The Research Library also has the biggest Theater Collection in the country, the first major sound archives open to the public and a unique Dance Collection.

"Our materials must be used here," Thor Wood pointed out, "and our stacks are closed. That's because we have a great deal of rare material like manuscripts, letters, prints, original scene and costume designs, posters. Of course, we have strong book collections, too and unlike other institutions, we save the ephemeral—things other people have thrown away like programs and photographs."

The Dance Collection contains the finest "dance print" collection in the country and the largest file of dance pictures in the world. Its manuscript material includes letters, diaries, notebooks and scrapbooks from the private files of famous dance personalities. Among the rare volumes the oldest is a unique manuscript of one of the earliest treatises on dancing, written about 1465-1475 in Italy by a dancing master named Giorgio e del Giudeo. The book describes social dancing of the time, as well as Giorgio's own ballet works and those of other great masters. Newest of the archival material is an oral history of taped interviews with some of the most important people in today's dance world, along with a filmed history of their work. Another project underway, the filming of current ballet repertoire, has been financed by a gift from choreographer Jerome Robbins in memory of his mother.

The film archives are meant to supplement dance scores just as phonograph records supplement the musical scores. "Some of the films in our file aren't very glamorous," said Genevieve Oswald, Curator of the Dance Collection. "Many of the older ones are only parts of ballets, some of them of dancers in rehearsal clothes, and some of them were filmed for TV in Germany. But now we're filming whole ballets from our current repertoire. Most of them are strictly for the scholar—we have no legal right to show them in public exhibition, but we hope to get some of those rights."

This Dance Collection doesn't serve only the United States—it fills requests from all over the world: a copy of a newspaper review or a photograph of a ballerina or an excerpt from a manual of ballet exercises written in St. Petersburg in 1904. The Rockefeller Foundation granted funds just for cataloging the thousands of miscellaneous items, and the Ford Foundation added another grant to use computers to amalgamate all the files. Besides the 26,000 books and pamphlets relating to dance, the Collection has a vast assortment of everything from librettos to original drawings. The flow of new material seems continuous: private gifts from the collections of the world's great dancers, from Massine to Ted Shawn of Jacob's Pillow.

But the Research Library is not just a library of sight—it is also a rare library of sound. The backbone is 200,000 recordings collected over the past forty years by Philip L. Miller, former chief of the Music Division. Miller built the collection through his own dedication: the drive of a man with a sense of history who knew that, someday, there must be archives of recorded sound and there would be a place to hear them. He persuaded record companies to give him sample copies of everything, and he searched out old, discarded recordings, some of which dated from 1890. The richness of history owes so much to quiet, determined men like Philip Miller.

Supplementing Miller's collection was a grant of $150,000 from the Rodgers and Hammerstein Foundation, as well as a donation of Richard Rodgers' personal noncommercial recordings. The overall archive of sound has been named after Rodgers and Hammerstein. It represents the entire range of recorded sound, from classical music to jazz to electronic sound, from old cylinders recording the golden age of opera to John Barrymore reading scenes from Shakespeare, from original cast recordings of Broadway plays to privately recorded performances of great singers and musicians—and everything else from bird calls to Congressional hearings. David Hall, the Head of the Archives, is now concerned with the need for another fund to put onto tape all the cylinder records, the piano rolls, the variable-speed recordings and the rare and fragile records.

Rivaling the quality of the other research division is the Theater Collection, whose Chief is Paul Myers. There is nothing comparable to it in this country and no collection so extensively used. These research rooms are areas where the silence is deep and the faces are of the old and the eager. Many of them are performers, those who have been and those who hope to be: a retired actor rereading a friendly review; a stage director searching old records for new ideas; a young actress who just wants to see what the young Katharine Cornell looked like. Or there might be a college student doing a research paper on clowns, or someone looking up the program of a forgotten play. The files are full of portfolios and playbills and scrapbooks and letters, as well as press books from hundreds of motion pictures with more than a million movie photographs.

What, then, is the key to this Library & Museum? Is it simply a place for the satisfaction

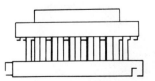

of curiosity? Is it just another element in the educational process? Is it primarily a place for leisure, for the entertainment of the mind and soul?

The answer, of course, combines all of these facets, but with the addition of an integral element: creativity.

This is a building where the sparks fly. A gifted child is enthralled by a piece of music. A playwright studies a working copy of a famous play. A composer in the Toscanini Memorial Archives pours over the original manuscript of a great composition. Greatness stirs greatness, and there is so much of it in the Library & Museum.

In the course of years more millions of people will move through this building, and many of them will be amused, reminded, broadened; but some will be stirred enough to create something out of their own imagination and talent.

The doors here are open free of charge to everybody for more hours a day and more days a year than at any other building in the Center.

And there isn't another Library & Museum like it anywhere in the world.

(1) Alexander Calder and his grandson watch the installation of the sculptor's "Le Guichet" in front of the Library & Museum of the Performing Arts, checking it with a model of the huge stabile.

(2) Part of "The Circus" exhibit at the opening of the Library & Museum, with Mayor Robert F. Wagner (*foreground*) and John D. Rockefeller 3rd looking on, and (3) a display of puppets in the Library & Museum's Children's Library.

1   SANDOR ACS

Among many delights in the Children's Library of the
Library & Museum, (1) one can select a book about
dancing, (2) find out how music notes are written
down, or (3) make a marionette move.

2
3

SANDOR ACS

SANDOR ACS

1

For adults, too, the Library & Museum offers a wealth of possibilities: (1) the open book shelves, (2) thousands of records to be listened to on individual audio sets, or (3) just a pleasant place to relax.

SOME RECENT ACQUI

ALISON AMES, THE NEW YORK PUBLIC LIBRARY   **1**
BETH BERGMAN   **2**

(1) The Research Library reading room in the Library & Museum.

(2) Rare manuscripts on display in the Toscanini Archives.

(3) Agnes de Mille, famed dancer and choreographer, and Dr. Robert Henderson, Chief of the General Library & Museum, look over a display of books about the dance.

3

the
metropolitan
opera

The opening of a new Metropolitan Opera House is not merely a Happening—it is the American musical event of a century.

They had waited a long time for this one, so they were all there—the aristocrats and the political leaders, the millionaires and the models, the grande dames and the wife of the President of the United States. Mrs. Lyndon Johnson later wrote Anthony A. Bliss, President of the Metropolitan Opera Association, "One cannot help but feel that it is the beginning of another Golden Age in the history of the Metropolitan Opera."

Things had come a long way since the day after a big storm in Montana when suave, lean Anthony Bliss had to put on a pair of spurs and climb a telephone pole to take an important call from New York. The call was from Wallace Harrison, architect of the Opera House, who had just come from a critical meeting with the other Lincoln Center designers. He reported to Bliss that the others felt the Opera House had to be lined up with the front of Philharmonic Hall and the State Theater, which would mean narrowing the House by thirty feet. "I'm in a corner here," Harrison told Bliss, "I know we'll eventually have to lose that space anyway because we won't have the budget to build it. But I wanted to see if it was all right with you."

Bliss, who was not in a corner but swaying back and forth on the telephone pole with no blueprints in front of him, felt forced to say, "If you think it will all fit, you're the architect, you're the boss."

Bliss and his fellow members of the Board of Directors had lived through forty-seven previous sets of plans for a new House. It was Bliss' father Cornelius, Chairman of the Board of the old Metropolitan, who had conceived the idea of organizing a nonprofit membership corporation to buy the old Met from the real estate company owning it. And it was Cornelius Bliss and Charles Spofford who in the 1930's first approached Mayor LaGuardia for his help in building a new Met. The old Opera House had nostalgia and charm, but only 2,600 of its 3,600 seats offered a full view of the stage. Furthermore its backstage facilities were so archaic there was no space to store scenery or hold rehearsals. Nor could it be air-conditioned, and it therefore stood empty all summer.

The old Met was new in 1883, when the Academy of Music on Fourteenth Street moved to its site on Thirty-ninth Street and Broadway. That happened simply because Mrs. William H. Vanderbilt was refused the use of the specific opera box she wanted at the Academy. She promptly recruited seventy families, who each contributed ten thousand dollars, and another opera house was soon under construction. It not only emerged as the largest auditorium in the world, but it had 122 boxes. "From an artistic and musical point of view," the New York *Post* complained, "the large number of boxes is a decided mistake." Mrs. Vanderbilt and her friends disagreed. Nor were they fazed by the critic who called it "that new yellow brewery on Broadway."

Opera boxes had been part of the American tradition since the country's first permanent opera house, the Theater St. Philippe in New Orleans, was built in 1808. Boxes there were latticed so that social celebrities could slip in without being recognized. The term "Diamond Horseshoe" came into being when a fire in 1892 caused the Met to be refurbished and the boxes were strung with electric lights. "Diamonds" could also have indicated the price of the boxes, one of which later sold for as high as $122,000. Each box was a socially important reception room. In 1907 Henry James wrote in *The*

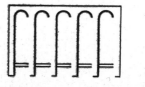

127

American Scene, "The opera . . . plays its part as the great vessel of social salvation, the comprehensive substitute for all other conceivable vessels. . . ."

Most of all, though, the Met meant music, the home of the finest opera in the world, sung by the greatest artists.

The plain-faced yellow brick exterior of the old Met hid a heart of plush and gold, but the Depression plunged it into a financial crisis. The hero was Cornelius Bliss, who formed the nonprofit corporation to buy the House, and the heroine was Mrs. August Belmont.

They call her "the woman behind the Met." A woman of great warmth and dignity, Eleanor Robson Belmont was once an actress celebrated on two continents. "To me, opera has always been sixty percent music and forty percent acting," she said. But it was the music that moved her most. She remembered the night when, after a long day at the Opera Guild, she went to hear *Le Nozze di Figaro*, sung by Pinza, Rethberg, Brownlee and Sayao. "I was alone, and after that beautiful performance, I had a feeling I was floating home in a state of spiritual exaltation. When I put my head on the pillow I cried to think that Mozart could not have heard his glorious opera as it was given that night, and the cheering that followed it."

It was more than her love of music, or even her money, that made Mrs. Belmont the grande dame of the opera; it was the force of her imagination and determination. During the Depression of 1933, she became the first woman Board member of the Metropolitan Opera Association. Financial prospects were so bleak that the Board discussed canceling the coming season. The small, fiery Mrs. Belmont told them, "This must not be."

She quoted an Italian proverb, "When you are desperate, look to the poor man, not to the rich." She founded the Metropolitan Opera Guild, membership open to everyone for minimal dues. She persuaded David Sarnoff of NBC to keep the Met on the air in a weekly radio program. For millions of Americans the opera on the air—with the mellifluous voice of announcer Milton Cross—became a Saturday afternoon ritual. Guild membership flourished. And through Mrs. Belmont and the Guild, more than one million students were given reduced price tickets to attend the Opera.

"That Mrs. Belmont, she's the best of them all," insisted Robert Moses, who does not always have kind words for everyone.

It was also Mrs. Belmont who strongly supported the need for a new opera house. The Metropolitan archives reveal new house plans dating from 1917. The first site considered has since become Radio City Music Hall. Architect Wallace Harrison has lived with the creation of such plans for almost half his lifetime. He smilingly tells how Charles Garnier, architect of the Paris Opera, studied his own problem for three or four years, spent another ten years developing his design—and resigned twenty-seven times during construction of the house.

Harrison had his own unique problems with the Met Board because a dramatic fight was brewing among its thirty members. Out of it would come a head-on collision of two contradictory concepts.

"We had a strong element on the Board that was wrapped in the gold-curtain nostalgia of the old Met and wouldn't even consider leaving it, and they formed an Old House Committee," Charles Spofford explained. "But we also had C. D. Jackson, publisher of *Time* magazine, and Irving Olds, then President of U. S. Steel, both very able, very powerful and very forward-looking fellows, and they spurred the idea of a New House Committee. Their argument was that it wasn't only uneconomic to run the Opera in the old house, but it wasn't even sanitary."

The New House won, but then came the arguments about the design and quality of the building.

"An opera house should not look like a bank, a jail or a drugstore," explained Harrison. "It should have a sense of both dignity and gaiety . . . as a home for grand opera, it should have grandeur."

The London *Times* agreed and editorialized, "As building materials have become more standardized, the tendency has grown for public buildings to look alike. It is not always easy for the visitor to tell from a distance whether he's approaching a hospital, a light engineering factory, or an open prison . . ." The *Times* then added, "It may be all right for a theater to tuck itself away in a side street, but there ought to be something opulent about a building for Opera."

"We tried countless shapes for the main house," said Harrison. "Round, square, wedge-shaped and many others. But, invariably, we came back to the classic Renaissance opera house." One of Harrison's earlier designs had a more contemporary tone, but the Board had said no.

"The bulk of opera is nineteenth century," explained Rudolf Bing, General Manager of the Met since 1950. "To put these works in an ultra-modern setting would be like mounting an old master in a new frame."

The final result was a compromise, a kind of modern baroque, mixing the old with the new—flowing lines, great spaces, repeated curves, claret-colored walls, crystal chandeliers. Giving it all a sweeping grandeur was the double staircase spanning the Grand Tier Promenade like a beautiful bridge. It had all the elaborate elegance of European opera houses yet still had a jewel-box feeling of intimacy.

Harrison had a staff of fifty working for three years on the final plans. One plan backed up the Opera House with a tall tower building that would have given Lincoln Center all the office and storage space it would ever need—but that was cut out because of budget. Also eliminated was a Piccolo Metropolitan, a complete reproduction of a small theater in Munich which was to be part of the Opera House.

Despite the reluctant surrender of all this space, the Met staff knew what they wanted. Rudolf Bing's Assistant Manager, Herman E. Krawitz, had toured European opera houses for ten weeks and returned with a number of specific recommendations. But more important than the specific was the general thesis: "We must not ask outsiders what our needs are—we know our own needs."

And what *did* they need?

Rudolf Bing had it all detailed, a long list based on sixteen seasons in the old Met:

A stage four times the size of the old one.

One stage on each side of the main one, permitting a complete change of scenery within two minutes.

A sound curtain to separate the main stage from the rear and side stages, allowing four rehearsals to take place simultaneously.

Enough space to store most of the sets and props needed for a full season.

The same kind of interior proportion and intimate feeling of the old House, with the same horseshoe-shaped auditorium.

An enlarged orchestra pit like the one he had known in Vienna, which many conductors had called the finest in the world. (At one time there were four conductors and a swarm of stagehands moving furniture around the old Met stage to determine the preferred size of stage and pit.)

Reginald Allen suggested a room for chorus rehearsal that could also serve as a recital hall. Herman Krawitz proposed layouts of the scenic studio and almost everything else, particularly in the backstage areas. Rudolph Kuntner, Director of Stage Operations, detailed his electrical and mechanical requirements, and these would ultimately make the Met the most modern and efficient opera house in the world. Commenting on all the backstage equipment, one foreign visitor remarked, "If God had had them, He could have created the earth in four days instead of six."

Some of the mechanical marvels included motorized wagons to bring scenes intact from the side stages; hydraulic lifts for raising whole scenes from below stage; elevators to add aprons to the stage, or raise the entire pit, or eliminate it; and the most elaborate lighting system of any theater in the world.

"We have our control room at the rear of the orchestra," said Rudolph Kuntner, "and we call it Cape Canaveral because our control-light panels cover three whole walls."

The lights work on code. A lighting operator can select one of four color slides for each of seventy-two spotlights automatically, or he can preset a combination in advance. In fact each stage light can be preset for twenty scenes. Famed lighting consultant Jean Rosenthal, the first

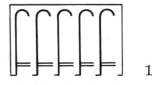

lighting designer in the Met's history, considered this light control vital, "because the emphasis on light has moved from illumination into part of the design aspect of the production."

The mechanical equipment is an even greater wonder. There are 105 pipes on which to hang scenery, and each pipe will hold 1,000 pounds. Push some buttons and you can make any pipe move as fast as 180 feet a minute. "This whole system was designed especially for us," added Kuntner.

"The new House gives more of a chance for inventive staging, especially with lifts, trapdoors and all these other things we didn't have before," said the renowned stage designer Cecil Beaton. "We couldn't have had those," he said, pointing to a grand staircase raised on stilts to be used in a ballroom scene. "Now we can roll them into place and lower them. A lot of people can unexpectedly come up from underneath. Anything to keep the audience alert is a help."

For one of the most fascinating vantage points where you can see it all, you must go to the very top of the Met, past a door that says, "There is no room beyond here." On the other side of that door are narrow slats of wood, on which you have to walk very carefully. And, through the spaces between the slats, you have an aerial view —the iron pipes, the enormous hanging scenery, and the singers on stage six floors below. Ten feet above one side of the stage sits the man in the booth waiting to push buttons.

So time-saving and efficient is all this push-button control that Herman Krawitz remarked, "We could even cut out the intermission if we wanted to."

That, however, is not something anyone would want to do. Intermission is a large part of the opera's social fun. It is the time to sip champagne or stare or small-talk. It is the time to stroll over the deep-pile, red carpet, to look at the portraits and sculptures of the famous singers in the downstairs lobby, time to step out onto the patio and absorb the atmosphere and the view.

Neither would they ever consider eliminating the box seats, as the Philharmonic had done. But, because of the gilt on the boxes, the Diamond Horseshoe has become the "Golden Horseshoe." The twenty-nine boxes are assigned to subscribers on the basis of seniority only.

The question of Met seats was a fundamental one. Should they have an opera house that packs in the largest possible number of people, or should they concentrate on getting the best acoustics? Some singers have voices large enough to fill any hall, but there are not many of them. Most of the European opera houses with the best acoustics have about 2,000 seats, but it just wasn't economically feasible for a house of that size to survive here. At one time, Wallace Harrison was asked to plan for a seating capacity of 6,000. The final compromise called for 3,800 seats, somewhat larger than the old Met. Unlike the old Met, however, even those people sitting in the last row of the Family Circle would have a full view of the stage and would be able to hear everything.

"In an opera house, everything has to be designed in terms of sound, because sound is the main reason to go to an opera," Harrison commented. "I could have experimented, I suppose. But the bigger the involvement, the less real room there is to experiment. You just can't experiment with 45 million dollars."

After studying the sound in the world's great opera houses and consulting the country's leading acoustical experts, Harrison concluded, "I still believe that acoustics is an art, not a science." Yet there were some standard acoustical devices to be employed: the proportionately narrow width of the house; the sloping proscenium; the pattern of domes for the ceiling; the wooden reflectors on much of the scenery; the air space between wall and concrete; the reflecting panels of wood from the West African Bubinga tree, thought to be especially adaptable to acoustical purposes. Even the tall chandeliers retract into the high ceiling so as not to deflect the sound.

The Lincoln Center Annual Report of 1960 estimated the cost of the new Met at $32 million. According to *Architectural Forum* magazine, that meant each seat would cost $8,421. But both figures were frequently revised, and always upwards.

"The trouble was that this sort of thing had never been done before, certainly not on this scale," noted John Drye, chairman of the New

House Committee. "If I had been told when we started how much money we would ultimately need, I'd have thought I was in with a bunch of nuts. There was a time when we were spending so much more than we had that I told Mr. Rockefeller, 'I couldn't go to jail with a finer bunch of fellows.'"

In the old days a Board member could ask how much money was needed, take a leisurely ride down to Wall Street, pay some courtesy calls on a number of firms and return with the required funds. But that was before construction costs became astronomical. In 1883 the old Met cost $1,732,478.71 to build (and that was twice its original estimate). The new Met would cost closer to $50 million. But the new Met was four times the cubic size of the old. If it could be stretched out on its side, it would be the equivalent of a 47-story building.

Lincoln Center had the responsibility of getting the building built and raising the initial money. The money came from everywhere—foundations, foreign governments, city, state and federal governments, as well as the multitude of music lovers, rich and poor. A half dozen high-school boys from a town in upstate New York sent a hundred dollars for a stage door in memory of a friend who had recently died. Residents of Wilton, Conn., put on a revue and raised enough money to endow several seats. The West German Republic gave $2.5 million to help buy stage equipment. A group of neighborhood children set up a lemonade stand and sent in their five dollars' profit to provide three feet of ballet practice-rail.

The site had long been cleared behind an eight-foot plywood fence. Gone were the decayed brownstones, the Green Gables Bar and the nearby sign, SPORTSWEAR, CORSETS AND GLOVES. Soon to arrive were 42,000 square feet of marble from the same Italian quarries that had supplied the stone for St. Peter's Basilica in Rome.

Before the bronze-and-glass facade was installed, a section of it was tested under severe wind pressure (with a vacuum behind it) in an abandoned hangar at the University of Miami. Some of the more complex stage machinery was checked at the University of Wisconsin. To provide the glitter the Met wanted, they ordered the world's largest installation of gold leaf—more than a million 3½-inch-square, tissue-thin sheets of 23-karat gold. And to get hand-detailed scalloping on the ceiling and the exterior of the boxes, it was necessary to seek out retired artisans who still remembered the nearly lost art.

There were 7,000 drawings detailing the final plans. Construction specifications filled five large volumes, each five inches thick. A statistician estimated that the completed building took 4½ million man hours. Nobody counted the aspirin.

"The shade of a red carpet and of a red nylon velvet wall may look the same, but when placed side by side they can be quite different," explained interior designer Edith Queller. "We examined several hundred samples of each material before we selected two that were harmonious."

Catalogue colors of paint were discarded, and hues were mixed on the spot to blend properly with the carpet or the paneling. Thirty different shades were created this way, using 15,000 gallons of paint.

The final touch came with the installation of thirty-two crystal chandeliers, including two eighteen feet in diameter—a gift from Austria.

"Preparing to open the new Metropolitan Opera House can be compared with the post-launching period and shakedown cruise of a great ship," remarked Anthony Bliss. "When opera houses one half its size were opened in Europe in the last few years, the resident companies needed as long as six months' preparation in advance of their opening."

The new Met had no such leeway. Four months prior to the actual opening night, Puccini's *The Girl of the Golden West* was given a test performance before 3,000 high-school students.

The first moments were dramatic. A technician came on stage and fired what looked like a blunderbuss and sounded like a nine-inch gun. That was to test the echo and decay rate of the sound. Then the orchestra played a loud chord and followed with the national anthem. Pacing in the back of the hall, peering at a noise-meter, and looking pale but determined was Wallace Harrison. After the first act Harrison emerged smiling.

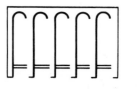

The Met decided that its opening opera must be both spectacular and American. It commissioned ranking composer Samuel Barber, and the result was *Antony and Cleopatra*. The new opera would become one of the most lavishly expensive productions ever done at the Met. Its cast of 400 requires 925 costumes (the costumes alone were budgeted at $200,000). A dozen complicated sets call for everything from a queen's barge floating down the Nile to a sea battle of epic proportions. For the staging the Met hired Franco Zeffirelli, whose recent productions had made him one of the most celebrated figures on the scene. On his first visit to the Met the excited Zeffirelli said, "What a house! I love gadgets, I love toys, and this house is a Cadillac!"

"The only sin in all theater is to bore," said Zeffirelli. "In opera you have to give everyone motion, because so much of the time, nothing happens. Singers only sing."

Many performers demonstrated sentiment and reluctance about moving from the old Met to the new one. Birgit Nilsson was sentimental enough to take two handfuls of stage dust on the closing night of the old House. "One handful is a memento for myself. The other is to strew on the stage of the new House, hoping that some of it will lodge in the cracks and help perpetuate the old Met's traditions." Miss Nilsson then smiled and added firmly, "Sentiment is no substitute for the ability to mount operatic productions with up-to-date equipment, or to provide more comfortable surroundings for the artists."

Tenor Jan Peerce had a similar view: "The Metropolitan is people: singers, stagehands, musicians, dancers, management, audience. This is the *real* Met. It's not being left behind on 39th Street."

"If one were to describe the inadequacy of the old theater in one phrase, it would be 'lack of space,'" continued Rudolf Bing. "In a new, big production, like *Aïda*, the limited margins on the sides of the stage were a maze that was nothing less than a hazard to limbs, lungs and lyricism. Let us not speak of the 'backstage area,' for there was none. There was Seventh Avenue instead."

Asked what he would miss most from the old House, the tall, slim, dignified Bing answered wryly, "The darkness of my old office. I haven't seen daylight in sixteen years."

Assistant Manager Francis Robinson added the footnote, "There is no rule that hardship is needed to create inspiration." And the general staff slogan seemed to be: "I'm weeping, but I'm packing."

The vast job of moving to Lincoln Center went off without breakage or theft. "The company moved with its traditions, its works of art and its people," said Krawitz.

The old Met art fitted in well with the new: Wilhelm Lehmbruck's graceful, six-foot bronze "The Kneeling Woman" at the top of the curving stairway on the Grand Tier; a buxom nude by Aristide Maillol on each side of the staircase; a group of murals by Raoul Dufy, originally done as scenery for Jean Anouilh's *Ring Around the Moon*. One set of the Dufy murals is on the walls of the Top of the Met Restaurant, while the others cover the walls of two large rehearsal rooms.

There are also two new paintings by Marc Chagall, the largest he's ever done. They tower over the promenade of the Grand Tier, facing the huge glass area that looks out on to Lincoln Center Plaza. The south panel is primarily red, with figures of yellow, blue and green; the north panel is primarily yellow, with subject figures in red, blue and green. Both paintings use motifs and symbols familiar in Chagall's work: floating figures, barnyard animals and musical instruments that lend a fairytale quality to an Oriental atmosphere. The north panel has everything from the Tree of Life to the New York skyline to King David and Orfeo. The south panel includes a church that looks like Paris' St. Germain des Prés and a gypsy that is said to look like Rudolf Bing. Both panels are dominated by musical images. The total effect is festive, gentle and dramatic.

The Met gave a second preview, five days before its formal opening, this time to an audience of 2,000 construction workers from the sixty-five unions who had helped build the House.

"A stonemason was in Mrs. C. V. Whitney's seat last night," Jimmy Breslin wrote. "And a group of carpenters came over from O'Boyle and

Mulvihill's Bar and sat down in David Rockefeller's box like it was nothing. And six members of Painter's Local 803 sat in the Parterre and discussed opera as they knew it. 'We were workin' the other day,' one of them was saying, 'you know, gold leafin' the ceiling, and here's this big opera broad, and I looked down and I yelled, "Hey, how do you like it, baby?" And you know what she said? She motioned something in Italian.' "

Backstage there were still problems. Even after rehearsals had begun, steel workers would still move in every night and continue welding until dawn. Besides that, there had been no time to test some of the new equipment. Wheels broke, motors stopped and the turntable wouldn't turn.

Page 6, Paragraph F, in one of the construction specification books noted for Job No. N-150-B, Section SE 63, Addendum No. 2: "Wagon and Turntable Structure shall be designed for static live loading of 125 pounds per square foot. Wagon shall be capable of moving 10,000 pounds, plus its own weight."

"The table had been built to carry 10,000 pounds," said Herman Krawitz, "and here we were, putting the whole Egyptian Army on it." It wasn't the whole army, but it was 333 members of the cast. That, plus a 22-foot-high sphinx weighing one and a half tons that had been built by Properties Construction man Richard Graham and his staff. The turntable was to permit whole sets to revolve swiftly and dramatically.

"When the turntable broke," said Reginald Allen, "we had to put a crew of nine stagehands inside the sphinx to turn it on a castered pivot. It worked okay at rehearsal, on an ordinary ground cloth. But before dress rehearsal, the stage was covered with a glossy gold cloth, and the men inside the sphinx just couldn't get up any traction." So the Metropolitan Opera soon received a bill for fifteen pairs of sneakers. Even that wasn't the end of the problem. The nine men inside the sphinx didn't know when to start and stop pushing. "So we had to put a conductor with a score inside with them, to cue them."

At the gala opening night Rudolf Bing met Mrs. James Price, mother of Leontyne Price—who was performing the role of Cleopatra. Mrs. Price, who had never met Mr. Bing before, remarked to him, "Mr. Bing, I've always envisioned you as a heavier man."

"Until a week ago, I was," he answered.

The night was September 16, 1966.

Among the stream of celebrated arrivals there was one man of special imagination. Handsomely dressed in white tie, he arrived in front of Lincoln Center in a hansom cab, helped out his lady and then watched the horse and cab clip-clop away, while the Rolls Royces behind him waited impatiently and perhaps a little enviously.

Inside, awaiting the opening-nighters, was the red, gold and ivory of the new Metropolitan Opera House, as well as the control booth with 3,190 light switches and the three bars stocked with 3,000 bottles of champagne. ("We'll never run out of champagne," said James Rogers. "It would be unthinkable.")

The first stirring moment was the singing of "The Star Spangled Banner" by the full audience.

Who knew about all the time it had taken to crate, ship and set up the three-ton "cycs" (cycloramas) used for day (white) and night (blue) backdrops?

Who knew that the steel girders inside the turntable were twisted too far out of shape to make repair feasible (and a new turntable would cost more than $200,000)?

Who knew about the nine sneakered men and the conductor pushing inside the Sphinx, or that most of the cast could seldom sit down because to do so might damage the delicate and expensive costumes?

Who knew that assistant electrician Bruce Katzmann really loved opera. "If I get bored or distracted, it could throw the whole system out of whack."

Almost no one in the audience knew, and this was not the time to be concerned. This was a moment in history: opening night of a new Metropolitan Opera House.

The two hundred standees had waited in line all week, sleeping on the ground and wearing buttons with the names of their favorite opera singers. Sixty-three-year-old Harry Phillip had been waiting in lines like this since he first saw *Aïda* in 1919. Louis Peres, who had closed his

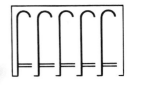

antique shop early in the week to join the line, said, "An opera house opens only once in a lifetime." Bruce Donelon, a nineteen-year-old student from Brooklyn, was first in line, and he was designated "Official Met Standee No. 1"; his white shirt was covered with homemade buttons saying, MOZART FOREVER. They had come with their transistor radios and camp stools and had made paper hats during the day to protect them from the sun.

For all of them, the Met was the most.

Of course the critics had also been waiting. A few had an assortment of complaints. The auditorium was an acoustic success and the stage facilities were stupendous, but they found fault with everything else, from the thickness of the rugs to the architecture.

But Harold C. Schonberg, of *The New York Times* commented, "Nobody these days can put up a building that is going to satisfy everybody. If it is modern, it will be damned by the intellectuals. If it is a compromise—and that is what the Metropolitan really is—it will call down the wrath of all sides. Nobody is going to like it except the public."

Perhaps the most enthusiastic audience member during that opening week was a visitor from Spain who was taken on a tour of the whole building before a performance. He was overwhelmed. All he could say was, "It's a *world!*"

It *is* a world. And it's a world in constant flux.

Referring to those critics who had never bothered to find out how a production develops, or what the collaboration is between producer, director, designer and conductor, and who had never attended any rehearsals or planning sessions, Rudolf Bing noted: "Picasso has the ability to draw a face like a photograph. If he chooses to distort it, that is done from a deliberate artistic point of view—but he still knows what a real face looks like. Some of our critics criticize results without knowing the reasons behind the face.

"Anybody who does not have to deal with it from morning to night simply cannot imagine the complications that arise from an elaborate opera being rehearsed during the day and another opera being scheduled for that evening. . . . All of this is further complicated by the fact that the soprano or tenor scheduled to sing that evening has sung the previous evening and therefore feels unable to attend that particular rehearsal. Or a singer falls sick, and another one has to be pulled out of an important rehearsal in order to step into a performance. . . . This is one of the most cruel professions, where abnormal vocal cords can bring you fame and fortune and where a sour note can ruin a career. We are dealing with people who, every night they stand on that stage, are fighting for their lives."

"One doesn't learn opera," Bing remarked, "one lives it."

In opera, as in anything else theatrical, there is no artistic decision that does not have financial implications, and vice versa. In 1967 the Metropolitan Opera published its first full financial report in ten years. It revealed that season as the most successful in the company's history, the longest and best-attended season and "possibly the most satisfying artistically." But it pointedly noted that while income had more than doubled, expenses had more than trebled.

"Opera, as produced on the scale of the Metropolitan's offerings, has never been self-supporting, and never can be," the report said. "The box office receipts for a night at the Metropolitan may bring in $42,000; it costs $59,000 to raise the curtain."

"This business is getting too big to run by passing the hat around," remarked George S. Moore, President of the Metropolitan Opera Board and former Chairman of the First National City Bank of New York. And, yet, hat-passing is vital. The Met currently operates on an annual deficit of more than $3 million, and this is expected to at least double in the coming years because of constantly increasing costs. To meet the recurrent crisis the Met is deeply dependent on many people. The 1967 report listed more than 650 individual patrons who annually give $1,000 or more, 85 corporate patrons annually contributing $2,500 or more, and the steady and generous contributions of a number of foundations. There are also such exceptional gifts as Eastern Airlines' contribution for a new production of Wagner's *The Ring of the Nibelungs,* Texaco's sponsorship of weekly radio broadcasts and the Ford Foundation's matching grant of $2.5 million for a ten-year development program.

"The world of opera is the world of unreality," said Mario Labroca, artistic director of the Teatro La Fenice in Venice. But the reality of the unreality is the hard, physical fact that the Metropolitan Opera has a permanent staff of more than 1,000 people and its 1968-69 expenses were $17.4 million.

Moreover, it costs $2.5 million each year to mount new productions of old classics. While it is true that the Met has averaged as high as 99 percent attendance in recent seasons, it is also true that this would have been still higher but for the few "non-traditional" operas. A production of the critically successful *Peter Grimes* caused one opera-goer in the old House to react so violently that she actually spat at the box office. "Playing to 28,000 people a week," said Bing, "we can't please everybody and we don't try. My job is to keep the Met alive and make it as good as I know how by producing masterpieces as seen through contemporary eyes, and to keep the Met's standard of singing high."

The Met is aware that it has a waiting list of some 10,000 people anxious to buy a subscription series, but it insists that this long list would diminish substantially if the Met embarked on new directions. While some new operas have been commissioned, such as Barber's *Antony and Cleopatra* and Levy's *Mourning Becomes Electra,* they have been few and infrequent.

The problems of opera selection have been multiplied by the lengthened season. In 1950 when Rudolf Bing succeeded Edward Johnson as General Manager, the Metropolitan's season was eighteen weeks long, and now it is thirty-one weeks; indeed it scarcely seems to end. In addition to the full season, there are the summer weeks in Central Park, the national tour, and a June Festival in the House.

Season planning is long-range, generally up to two years in advance. The jet plane has given the great opera singers to the world, and they must be sought out and signed. So must the best directors and designers.

The General Manager and his artistic staff meet almost daily to discuss scheduling and casts. These discussions are drawn out and deliberate, because there are several negotiating factors needed to attract top artists. Besides the money offered, the enticing plums for singers are opening night, new productions, premieres and broadcasts.

"If Miss Leontyne Price had a new production this year," said Assistant Manager and Artistic Director Robert Herman, "we want to see that Miss Nilsson, or Miss Sutherland, or Miss Tebaldi, or somebody else has one next year." Herman is acutely conscious of such things, because he's the man who arranges contracts with singers, conductors, musicians and dancers.

And there are innumerable other considerations. "We advance step by step," Herman noted. "First we consult a chart of operas and the seasons they were performed. If we see an opera such as *The Magic Flute* with a large empty space—which means it hasn't been played for too long a time— then we seriously consider it. We may also decide that a certain opera needs a complete restaging. But we can only afford three or four new productions a season, and these new productions must stand a fair chance of lasting eight or ten years. It's taken almost fifteen years to refurbish most of our repertory, and if we spend a lot of money on a loser that nobody wants to see again, then it really sets us back. On the other hand, an opera like *Don Carlo* can hardly be improved upon, so all we have to do is keep it clean and mended.

"We do perform in four languages, and we try to maintain some kind of balance, even though our repertory is primarily Italian. Anyway, there seems to be a real lack of Wagnerian singers, and French, too."

As Artistic Director, Robert Herman also maintains a chart of artists' availability. A straight red line indicates unavailability. Straight blue means they're available, and wavy blue means they're available for rehearsal. Still another of Herman's charts refers to rehearsal and

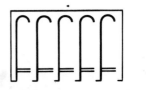

135

performance: pink (piano rehearsal); green (full orchestra); and a variety of colors for different subscription series.

Each of the eighteen subscription series must get an equal chance to see the new productions and new leading artists. The Met also makes a serious attempt not to present the same opera for the same subscription series two years consecutively.

And everyone, of course, wants to see the current stars, particularly when they try a new role.

"It took me seventeen years to sing in *Aïda*," said Richard Tucker, who has sung at the Metropolitan for a generation with a repertoire of some thirty operas. "I just wasn't ready for that role, vocally speaking. I just wasn't ready for what the role demands, and what the public demands. In fact, this is the first time I'm singing *Pagliacci*. They wanted me to wear Caruso's costume, but I'm afraid it wouldn't fit. A singer has to know, deep within himself, when the roles fit, too. Because once you've done a certain role, you can never go back in something less than that. After *Otello*, for example, vocally there's no other challenge. That's what I tell all the young singers: Guide yourself carefully, don't be too much an eager-beaver in what you think you can do."

Birgit Nilsson agrees. "Singers should not try to do more than they can do because there's always the real danger of hurting one's voice. I did it and survived, but how many do? Everybody has to make his own mistakes."

But that, too, is part of the responsibility of the Metropolitan's staff—to help decide which singers are ready for which roles, even in the smaller parts. The lovely young mezzo-soprano Judith Forst was one of those singers who had come to the Met by way of regional auditions held annually around the country. Assistant Manager John Gutman administers the audition program, among many other things, including the ballet and the Opera Studio. The Studio trains promising young singers and offers good teachers, tough rehearsals and the exposure of recitals, particularly at schools. Judith Forst was one of the few

to be able to jump the Studio transition and be signed up directly with the Met, a chance that comes to only one in several thousand.

"The first time I stepped on the Met stage was when I played the part of a page in *Rigoletto*," Miss Forst recalled. "I only had two dozen words, but I thought I'd die.

"But then you watch the big artists, and they really help. A young singer can drop a line on stage and feel as if their world is falling in, but these established artists can forget a line and never get flustered, just stay real cool and go on to the next.

"As soon as we're assigned to a part," she explained, "we have a coach upstairs to rehearse us in it. And it isn't just our own part; we're all assigned as 'covers' for different roles. Even if you're third or fourth 'cover' for a role, you always have to be ready because you never know when you're going to go on. Somebody gets sick or gets released for an outside engagement, and suddenly you're pushed up. For a leading role, there can be as many as eight 'covers,'"

Milko Sparemblek's thirty-eight ballet dancers in the Met are also always ready and waiting, grateful for the few operas that demand dancing. Conductor Herbert von Karajan drafted some of the dancers as Rhine maidens in his highly personal production of Wagner's *Das Rheingold*. In the first scene he has three of them seemingly swimming in the Rhine River, disappearing behind rocks and popping out of fissures, singing most of the time. But the voices actually come from three choristers crouched near a microphone inside a rock cave, where they closely watch a tiny TV set for von Karajan's baton cues. Meanwhile two ballerinas above them are strapped to a pair of hand-pulley elevator stands, while the third hangs on a higher portable boom. Also hidden behind the stage rock are the stage hands who do all the hoisting and hauling. The ballerinas are let down into the cave openings at the same time the singers are pulled up.

"It's not easy, said Lillian Sukis, who sings Woglinde. "We're timed to the split second."

The Metropolitan Opera chorus regards itself mainly as background rejoicing in the few chances to shine. "*Peter Grimes* is our favorite piece," declared Stella Gentile, who has been with the chorus for almost forty years. "The chorus is the real villain. We're the ones who drive the tenor crazy. He has to kill himself to get away from us. It's a strenuous opera with all that running around and the constant singing, but it's a virtuoso piece for the chorus."

Tall, blond William Zakariasen, a tenor, has the extra job of *screaming*. "Most of the leading singers don't want to do it themselves. It's bad for the voice. So when they take Cavaradossi offstage and torture him, I do the yelling. I make my vocal production match whoever's singing. For Konya I make it dark and German and throaty, for Corelli I make it bright and Italian. They thought about making me scream for Regina Resnik in *Electra,* but she wanted to do it herself. I get paid extra for it."

The chorus master is Kurt Adler, a big, heavy-jowled, calm man. "One must be calm here," he remarked quietly. "Excitement is an occupational disease and it kills."

The *Oxford Companion to Music* estimates that 42,000 operas and operettas have been written since the first opera production by a group of amateur actors in sixteenth-century Florence. That was Peri's *Dafne.* Most of those operas, of course, have slipped quietly into the woodwork of forgotten history, but periodically the Met management reaches into that woodwork to give its audience a fresh production of an old opera never before seen at the Metropolitan.

"When a new production is scheduled, I study recordings of the work, review accounts of old productions and research the libretto in an attempt to anticipate problems before they arise," said energetic Herman Krawitz, who wears two Met hats, Business Manager and Production Manager. "Pitfalls in estimating the budget for any production are unexpectedly long rehearsals and complicated scenic changes, not always evident in a design blueprint. Difficult scene changes required while the music plays on create additionally taxing problems and costs." (The original concept of Samuel Barber's *Vanessa* required a four-minute lull while the curtain was

down in Act III for a scene change. Krawitz persuaded Barber to write four minutes of music to appease audience impatience. (Barber later referred to that music as "The Krawitz Interlude.")

But before a new production can be budgeted and programmed, it must be created, designed and completely detailed. Nathaniel Merrill and Robert O'Hearn took more than a year to stage and design Richard Strauss's almost forgotten *Die Frau ohne Schatten.* They took even more time with a new production of *Boris Godunov*—which was made possible by a $300,000 grant by Mrs. DeWitt Wallace, co-chairman of the Reader's Digest Association. For the first time at the Met *Boris* would be sung in the original Russian.

For such productions Merrill and O'Hearn not only discuss the opera in terms of a fresh approach, but they read everything written about the work and the era. They usually search out original sources for settings and costume, and if possible, visit the original site of the scene.

After the creation comes the enormous detailing. "I find myself making dozens and dozens of lists of all kinds," Merrill commented. "But the great thing is that O'Hearn and I are practically neighbors and so we can constantly discuss even the smallest problems." Merrill went on to explain the toy soldiers set up on large sheets of blueprint draped over his dining room table. It was for *Der Rosenkavalier,* Act III. "They're perfect to use because their scale corresponds to a five foot person in relation to this blueprint of the set. This way I know exactly how many people I can get onto a stairway or through a doorway. And when I go into rehearsal, every move by every chorister has been plotted in detail, written down and marked exactly in each rehearsal score. I am sure there are other ways of working, but for me it's the only way."

Merrill believes that opera should be choreographed the way it sounds, translating musical patterns into visual patterns. "Take the fight in Act II of *Meistersinger.* It looks chaotic only because every movement of every chorus member has been carefully planned. The first pillow is

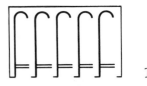

137

thrown in the air precisely at measure 41 of that section—it's marked in the scores. David hits Beckmesser right on measure 71 because the sopranos scream at high C. Of course, the movement is accompanying the music; but I want it to look the reverse—as though the music is coming out of the action spontaneously. If I could get that to happen 100 percent of the time, I would be a genius!"

Still young men, Merrill and O'Hearn have worked long enough with the Met to know the potential use of all the push-button mechanics and all the possible lighting patterns. They discuss lighting with bustling Rudolph Kuntner, who has 10,000 lamps on the bridges overlooking the stage.

They also confer with chief prop man Richard Graham whose shop turns out all the "hand props"—goblets, fans, a violin made of fiberglass. Such items as ornate Venetian columns constructed of urethane foam are produced under the supervision of Staff Designer David Reppa. On the wonders of urethane foam Reppa commented, "It comes in all thicknesses, and you can cut it into any shape or size you want. . . . That's what made it so good for these Venetian columns. It's also perfect for making the bark on trees."

And it makes handy clubs for the giants in *Das Rheingold* to use in hitting each other over the head. It is also used for masks, castle walls and flower pots.

The men of the Prop Shop must be ready to build anything from a bull ring to a witch's house to a miniature copy of the dome of St. Peter's Basilica—which is seen from the distance in the last act of a new production of *Tosca*.

"There's nothing we don't do except counterfeit money," said Ralph Picone. He was upholstering a set of eighteenth-century French furniture for *Adriana*, and explained: "We use rubberized hair. It's real hair sprayed with rubber. Gives you a little bounce."

Costumes are generally more expensive than sets, and the designer must have frequent and detailed discussions with Head Costumer Maureen Ting. Miss Ting has been with the Met for ten years, having worked previously with the Shakespeare Festival in Canada and the Old Vic in London. After seeing the designer's sketches and discussing his preferred colors and patterns, Miss Ting sends her assistant, Charles Kaine, to search the market for fabric swatches. Before Herman Krawitz arrived at the old Met, most of the tailoring and wig-making was contracted for outside, but now most of it is done within the Met. Preparing costumes for a new production may take six months to a year—particularly since several productions may be in work simultaneously. During one year when there were nine new productions, Miss Ting and her staff of forty tailors and dressmakers worked thirteen hours, six days a week, and nine-to-five on Sunday.

"A single chambermaid in *Der Rosenkavalier* has a costume including a petticoat, a skirt, an outer corset, an apron, a blouse, a drape and a beribboned hat," said Miss Ting. Each member of the cast, from the chambermaid to the star, comes for at least one fitting and often more. Identical costumes must be made for the lead and his replacement. "If you fit for the tall, thin one, it's often the short, heavy one who goes on," she said. "We try to have a costume ready for a stand-in for each production but then there's not always the same stand-in for each night, either. This may add up to some ten people for whom you've got to make about twenty-five sets of costumes." For *Boris Godunov* Miss Ting needed to make about 600 costumes.

"A historical costume must have deep folds," she continued, "and it must look like a museum painting. Synthetic fabrics are strong, but they're lightweight and just float around. That's why we often use upholstery fabrics for our costumes. We make a costume to last ten years, sometimes twenty. And when you see one of our singers wearing something that's supposed to be rags, it's probably made out of raw silk. The silk has an open weave to it, and we dip it and dye it within an inch of its life and break it up with a cheese grater to get that really authentic raggedy effect."

The Costume Department keeps bolts of cloth from the original costume material, in case somebody tears something and needs a patch. They also keep everything from fake fur to

138

heavy antique gold trimmings to a closet full of all types of shoes—for emergency use and last-minute replacements.

Several doors away are the wigmakers. They find that the best hair seems to come from Italy where the women have a simple, healthful diet and don't go in for bleaches and rinses as much as elsewhere. But with the renewed popularity of wigs for women, the price of hair has risen sharply.

After the artists have been costumed and wigged, after the props have been planned and shaped, then come the rehearsals.

Since there are so many different operas produced in a single week, and since many other operas are always in different stages of preparation, the scheduling of rehearsals requires complicated logistics. That huge headache belongs to Frank Paola, Musical Secretary and Company Manager. Paola keeps an oversized record book in which everything that will happen in the Opera House is itemized: the hour and place of rehearsals, the amount of time needed and the number of people involved for each, the cast changes for a work's various performances, additional rehearsals for new cast members. There are rehearsals for lead singers, for supporting performers, for groups, for orchestra, for ballet, for chorus. Paola is in charge of a logistical timing that must be exquisite in its precision.

Paola also must find time to arrange the company's tours. This involves the transport of some 300 people, plus all the equipment needed for seven operas. Two chartered jet planes are used.

As far as staff and cast are concerned, some of the intimacy of the old Met has gone, simply because the new House now has so much going on that was never before possible. But at the same time, the display of artistic temperament has been minimized because more artists have the space and comfort they require. Some singers, however, are distressed about the air conditioning and have the stage ducts closed during their performances. A few, wary of the effect of piped air on their voices, even keep their dressing room windows open during the hot summer.

Richard Hauser's men, who handle the props on stage and must sometimes make changes within seven seconds, have no such complaints about air conditioning or the loss of intimacy. During hectic periods they may work up to sixteen hours a day, hardly ever leaving the building for lunch, and sometimes sleeping on mattresses in the office. They also handle the general maintenance of the hall, strike sets and put up the new ones. Keeping chandeliers cleaned, repairing the scratched bronze in elevators, patching the terrazzo floor torn up by women's shoe heels is the concern of an executive stage manager such as Osie Hawkins. Most of these men on the Technical Staff have been with the Metropolitan for a long time, and they know their business well. They feel a deep pride in the organization and the new House, but it is not unmixed with some sentimentality about the old Met.

Even Maestro Fausto Cleva, one of the Metropolitan's most highly respected conductors readily says, "I must admit, I love the new Met. The sound is so much better. The sound comes up like a wave, no matter where you sit. And the beat is so much clearer. You can hear every detail. That means the music has more charm. In the old House, there were spots where the sound was dead."

For one of the Assistant Conductors—a man the audience almost never sees—the improved sound is also a great benefit: He is the prompter.

"Most people think a prompter is strictly for the words," said William Weibel, who formerly held the post. "They couldn't be more wrong. What singers need least are the words. What they need most are the musical cues. They need to know when to 'attack.' Give a wrong cue and the singer comes in wrong and ruins everything. Timing is the complete key."

The Met's prompter resides in a little box at the center of the stage. His work area is about thirty-six inches wide, but it has a stairway, a tall stool, a tiny TV screen, two padded arm rests, a rug, and a telephone—all the comforts of home. A prompter learns to modulate his voice so its just loud enough for the singers to hear him, but soft

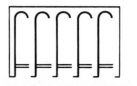

139

enough so that the audience doesn't. When the singers are too far away to hear him, he uses hand signals.

These cues are particularly critical when a "cover" must come in quickly to replace a singer who is ill. A cover is asked to be within twenty minutes of the theater at any time during a performance, and must be physically, vocally and mentally prepared. During a flu epidemic one year, Nicolai Gedda suddenly felt sick and canceled his appearance as Rudolfo in *La Boheme*. His cover, Luciano Pavarotti, sang two acts, then got dizzy and started to stagger. Still another cover, Barry Morrell, had to come in and sing the last two acts.

Occasionally these crises cause awkwardness, but the Met has learned to cope with it. It has also learned how to cope with audience members who arrive late.

Latecomers are sent to a side room to watch the opera on closed-circuit television until the first intermission. This is not to punish them but to protect the rights of those who arrived on time. At first there were several hundred latecomers to each performance, but that number has dwindled to an average of twenty or thirty. One late arrival was so furious at not being admitted into the auditorium that he tore up his libretto and kicked over and broke a piece of statuary. He was arrested and was brought to court hoping for a sympathetic judge. Instead the judge said, "What are you, some kind of nut? I was late to *my* favorite opera and *I* didn't break anything." The judge ordered him to pay for the damages.

Subscribers to the Met in New York feel a strong proprietory interest in the House—as they should. They form the financial backbone of the Metropolitan's season. The Met, of course, could presell every seat, but for each performance it holds a minimum of 400 seats for the general public and it has as many as eighteen nonsubscription performances in a single season. Almost every performance sells out soon after tickets go on sale, and there are nearly always standees.

Though Dr. Samuel Johnson decided a long time ago that opera was "an exotic and irrational entertainment" and Carlyle and Tolstoy both thought opera a waste of time, Walt Whitman said of its inspiration, "But for opera, I could never have written *Leaves of Grass*." And now throughout the United States there are more than 750 professional and nonprofessional opera companies who give more than 4,000 performances during an average year.

The Metropolitan commands the largest audience for the longest season of any opera company in the country. Yet each season is a financial hazard. Unlike the Paris Opera or London's Covent Garden or Milan's La Scala, the Met gets no government subsidies. In these days of soaring costs even Mrs. August Belmont reluctantly accepts the idea that government subsidy for opera may soon be necessary.

But there is a larger question that the Met must resolve: How long can the foliage flourish without more new roots? How long must the Metropolitan serve mainly as the stage for long-dead composers? What is the future of a museum?

Rudolf Bing has no qualms about facing up to any of these questions. He sees the Met as a *living* museum presenting fresh productions of the classics. New operas, he feels, should be tested by other companies for whom the financial and professional risks are less crucial. Out of this vital experimentation the cream would ultimately come to the Metropolitan.

"I don't feel that to do new operas for the sake of new opera is valid," Bing insisted. "It's not fair to the Met's public to test new composers on them. I don't believe in undiscovered genius or undiscovered great works."

Bing's successor, 53-year-old Goeran Gentele has a different view. The former general manager and director of the Royal Opera House in Stockholm believes that the Met *must* modernize, *must* experiment, *must* break with tradition.

"We must of course have the classics, the evergreen," said the slim, ruddy-faced former actor, who still directs movies and opera. "But you must also follow your time, express it. If you go against it, it will run over you. I want to commission new works here, I want to experiment and use all of Lincoln Center."

Gentele directed *Aniara*, some years ago, a story set on a doomed space ship with a partly electronic score. "We played it over a hundred times and now it seems like a classic." Gentele also used a laser beam for the first time on any opera stage. And one of his Royal Opera productions, *The Journey*, used films as well as a rock band in the pit along with the opera orchestra.

"I'm a modern man," said Gentele. "We must not forget that opera is a folk art like bullfighting and prizefighting . . . opera is theater, and acting must be as important as singing . . . opera must be for everyone. . . ."

However strange and new all this sounds coming from a general manager of the Met, it somehow fits in with something said by the grand and remarkable Mrs. Belmont:

"My main wish for the Met of tomorrow is that it will not only be the showcase for the best of the past, but that it will also produce some of the fresh new things—no matter what their initial success—to help shape the taste of the future."

The old Metropolitan Opera House, which stood at 40th Street and Broadway.

(1) The new Metropolitan Opera House at Lincoln Center during construction.

(2) Mrs. August Belmont, the grande dame of the Metropolitan Opera Association.

(3) Anthony A. Bliss, former President of the Metropolitan Opera Association, presides over a meeting. Also attending are Robert Herman (*left*) and Herman Krawitz, Assistant Managers, and Rudolf Bing (*partially hidden*), General Manager.

(4) Opera buffs lined up for the first day of ticket sales at the new House in Lincoln Center.

2   EUGENE COOK

3   THE NEW YORK TIMES

4

LOUIS MÉLANÇON, FOR THE METROPOLITAN OPERA

The new Metropolitan Opera House.

(1) Rudolf Bing, for 22 years the General Manager of the Metropolitan Opera.

(2) Conductor Thomas Schippers at a rehearsal for the opening night performance, the premiere of Samuel Barber's *Antony and Cleopatra*.

(3) On opening night of the new Metropolitan Opera House, director Franco Zeffirelli embraces Leontyne Price, who sang the starring role of Cleopatra. Justino Diaz (*center*) co-starred as Antony, and Rosalind Elias sang the role of Charmian.

2

3

1

(1) Ponchielli's *La Gioconda* in a new production
designed by Beni Montresor, with Cornell MacNeil
(*center*) as Barbaba.

(2) A backdrop for the new *La Gioconda* being painted
in the Metropolitan's scenery shop by Vladimir
Odinokov (*left*) and two assistants, Elizabeth Matta
and Edward Burbridge.

(1) Saint-Saens' *Samson et Dalila*, with Rita Gorr and James McCracken in the title roles.

(2) Bizet's *Carmen* with Grace Bumbry as Carmen and Justino Diaz as Escamillo.

(3) Gounod's *Faust* with Gabriella Tucci as Marguerite and Nicolai Gedda as Faust.

1

2

3   LOUIS MÉLANCON, FOR THE METROPOLITAN OPERA

LOUIS MÉLANCON, FOR THE METROPOLITAN OPERA   **1**

LOUIS MÉLANCON, FOR THE METROPOLITAN OPERA   **2**

(1) In the new House, the Costume Department gained the space to make jewelry for Met productions.

(2) Puccini's *Tosca* with Birgit Nilsson in the title role, Franco Corelli as Cavaradossi, Gabriel Bacquier (*right*) as Scarpia, and Russell Christopher as Sciarrone.

(3) Aristide Maillol's sculpture "Summer" in the lobby of the Metropolitan Opera House after intermission.

(4) Goeran Gentele (*right*), General Manager-elect of the Metropolitan Opera, with Rudolf Bing, General Manager.

3

4

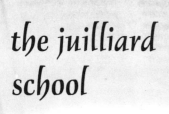

the juilliard
school

"I'll play until my fingers bleed."
—Student overheard in elevator at
The Juilliard School.

The pretty blonde with the sensitive face made the statement simply, without drama. It was something she accepted as the price of realizing her talent.

"Talent is a mysterious thing," noted the celebrated teacher of violin, Ivan Galamian, who has been at Juilliard since 1946. "Nobody can define talent. It is within you or it is not. People with smaller talent can work harder and make it bigger, but there is a limit. But if the talent is big, then it deserves the hardest practice. It deserves everything."

The 750 students at Juilliard get everything.

"With its move to Lincoln Center, The Juilliard School has become the most impressive conservatory in the entire world, with facilities at its disposal that no other conservatory can match," wrote Harold C. Schonberg in *The New York Times*. Schonberg went on to describe it as "the Taj Mahal of conservatories, opulent, beautiful, domineering—and big."

John W. Drye, Jr., a Juilliard Trustee and member of the Board, once asked why the building had to be so big and elaborate, and he was told that actually they felt they were "crowding a University into a shoebox."

The Juilliard School is the first major independent professional school in the United States dedicated to the teaching of all the performing arts. It has always been regarded as the best of the two dozen great music schools in this country, but gradually, it has also incorporated three more schools: drama, dance and opera.

The building, however, seems hardly a shoebox—it's a city-block wide and almost twice as long, second in size at the Center only to the Metropolitan Opera House. But it is still considerably smaller than originally planned.

"I made sixty-five different sets of plans for Juilliard," said the architect, Pietro Belluschi. His first proposal was for a fifteen-story building. "Then our budget got tighter and tighter and the building got smaller and smaller," Belluschi

recalled. Several floors and a dormitory were eliminated.

"After that, it was like pulling a sore tooth," added Belluschi. "We cut out a lot of architectural details that hurt at the time, like some nice wood paneling, and skimping on some walls, but in the long run, it was all to the good because there was less gilding on the lily."

Philip Hart supervised construction details on behalf of Juilliard, and one of his right-hand assistants was a young, talented scenery and lighting expert and teacher, Sidney Bennett. It was Bennett who first noted that a two-foot-square column was planned for the middle of the main traffic path between the scene shop and the performing area. The architects carefully explained that the column was absolutely essential. But after considerable sound and fury, the column was replaced by a 60-foot I-beam, one of the biggest interior beams in the city. Before it was encased in asbestos, Philip Hart gratefully wrote on it in chalk, BENNETT'S BEAM.

The Juilliard building is unique at Lincoln Center in that it is set apart from the rest of the buildings and is connected to the main plaza by a wide overpass. But in addition to that, it has its own distinctive quality. Belluschi has given the place a personal identity even though the exterior is of travertine marble like the rest of Lincoln Center.

The open entrance court, several stories high, acts as a dramatic architectural focus for the building. Another focus in the foyer of the Juilliard Theater is a sculptured wall almost fifty feet long and eight feet high. This "Nightsphere-Light" by Louise Nevelson is a moody expanse of shadowed abstract forms. Nearby is an abstract sculpture by Nagare, a gift of Japanese businessmen.

There are four auditoriums in the building. The Juilliard Theater has 1,000 seats so skillfully sectioned off by railings that the large, oval-shaped area has a comfortable intimacy. The Paul Recital Hall is a cherry-wood theater with 292 seats; it has a stage wall of organ pipes, and no backstage facilities. The Drama Workshop has a

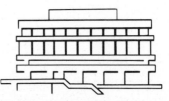

theater of similar size, a simple semicircle for working students. And then there is the dramatic Alice Tully Hall, operated by Lincoln Center, Inc., for the general public. The Chamber Music Society is housed there.

Alice Tully Hall is one of the gems of Lincoln Center. Half the size of Philharmonic Hall (it seats 1,096), it was designed to acoustic perfection by Heinrich Keilholz, who later handled the final acoustic work at the Philharmonic. The sound here is rich and clear—each instrument clearly defined, not a note lost, not a tonal shading dissipated.

The *New York Magazine* story describing the acoustic triumph and the hall's warm, colorful interior was headlined:

I LOVE YOU, ALICE B. TULLY

It was Alice B. Tully whose gift made the hall possible. Miss Tully, the granddaughter of the founder of Corning Glass, has had a fourteen-year career as a dramatic soprano of international reputation. Currently serving on the Boards of Directors of Juilliard, the New York Philharmonic and Lincoln Center, Inc., she remarked, "My one regret is that Tully Hall wasn't here when I was still singing."

Miss Tully herself chose the colors for the hall. "I wanted it to be a tranquil place, serene, relaxing, comfortable. I did not want anything to distract the listener in his seat from the music on the stage." And to make sure there was enough comfort for the longest legs, she invited a friend who was six-feet-four-inches tall to come and sit in various parts of the auditorium.

Throughout the Juilliard building it is evident that the design was carefully keyed to the needs of young people studying the performing arts. To minimize the transmission of sound, for example, the floors and walls float free, and some of the walls are twenty inches thick. To help the acoustics and perhaps to mitigate the boxed-in feeling in the more than eighty small practice rooms, the walls are slanted. In the Juilliard Theater electronically controlled jacks can raise or lower the ceiling seven feet to help meet acoustical requirements (up for opera, down for drama).

Everything is theatrically handsome upstairs: classrooms with picture windows, wall-to-wall carpeting, a luxurious student lounge and cafe-

teria, spacious studios, an art gallery, three baroque organs in their own white-walled rooms and the two-story Lila Acheson Wallace Library, where audio equipment is as common as blackboards.

"If I wanted to be reserved," remarked Peter Mennin, President of The Juilliard School, "I'd say it's all merely fantastic."

But there is a money problem. While the Juilliard building was built and paid for by Lincoln Center, Inc., the operating budget is Juilliard's responsibility—and the budget is several times what it was in the old building.

The old building on Claremont Avenue near Columbia University had grown out of two schools: the Institute of Musical Art, founded in 1905 by James Loeb and Frank Damrosch, and the Juilliard Graduate School, begun in 1924 in the old Vanderbilt mansion through the legacy of a textile manufacturer, Augustus D. Juilliard. The two combined in 1946 as The Juilliard School of Music.

The school developed and changed under each of its successive Presidents, John Erskine (1928-37), Ernest Hutcheson (1937-45) and William Schuman (1945-62).

Schuman's changes were perhaps the most significant. He was the one who expanded the Juilliard curriculum and included a Dance Division. And it was he who persuaded Lincoln Center, Inc., to include Juilliard. When Schuman left Juilliard to become President of Lincoln Center, Peter Mennin became Juilliard's new President.

Like William Schuman, Mr. Mennin is a composer of international reputation. He has written seven symphonies and many other concert works. Mennin's first association with Juilliard was as a teacher of composition in 1947.

"We all know major artists who trained beautifully but were not prepared for the concert stage," he commented. "We want to take the students with special talent and prepare them for the professional world."

Juilliard's standard of excellence demands driven talent, enormous discipline and unfailing courage. The talent is unquestioned. All the students know why they are here. The discipline is rigid and incessant—the small practice rooms are seldom empty and are often in use on Sundays. The courage is not only the kind that accepts bleeding fingers; it is stubborn persistence in spite of a creative artist's unsure place in an unsure world.

What is the future of a flutist in a country where more than a hundred symphony orchestras have gone out of business in the past six years? How many communities want a resident string quartet? How many jobs are there for opera singers, dancers, actors? And how many commissions are there for an original composition?

What students at Juilliard do know is that their degree gives them enormous prestige and easier entrée into the musical world. It is no secret that 85 percent of the major musical awards in this country are won by Juilliard students. So the conviction of these students is that if any musicians can successfully make it, those from Juilliard have the best chance.

That is why the waiting list is long, and that is why the admissions administrators are so selective.

The admissions test is an audition before a jury of faculty members—each trying to sense the potential artistry in the undeveloped talent. A simple majority vote decides entrance. Out of more than 750 applicants to the music school each year, approximately 170 are accepted. And they come to Juilliard from all over the world: Of the 650 music students an estimated 20 percent are from foreign countries.

"You must have an instinct about pupils and their talent, but it is so difficult to pick and choose," observed Florence Page Kimball, who has worked under all the Presidents of Juilliard in her distinguished career as a teacher of voice. "When somebody asks me, 'Do you have any more Leontyne Prices?' I tell them I didn't know I had Leontyne Price when she came." Leontyne Price has been her student for the past twenty years.

"I must work from the foundation, from the beginning of a talent," Miss Kimball said. "I can't accept well-established artists who feel they need a little freshening up."

The teacher-student relationship at Juilliard is at the core of the school's quality. It's an intimate relationship based on deep respect.

Juilliard's faculty are not simply teachers—they are master teachers, master musicians, master performers. Most of them have a background of significant accomplishment in the concert halls of the world.

Sascha Gorodnitzki is a renowned pianist and teacher. He was a student at Juilliard in the 1920's, and has been on the faculty since 1948. Gorodnitzki tells of one recent student who came for her lesson with her fingers taped. "I guess I overdid it," she told him, "I practiced eleven hours yesterday." Gorodnitzki discourages such intensity, but he himself remembers practicing ten hours a day for ten days to prepare for a competition. One of Gorodnitzki's prize students now is Albert Lotto, who has won a number of important international competitions. "But he doesn't push me," Lotto said. "He lets me decide when I am ready. Our relationship has been invaluable to me."

"We try to tell our students that we do not want to provide a sheltered atmosphere," remarked piano teacher Adele Marcus. A Juilliard scholarship student when she was fifteen, Miss Marcus won several international prizes and still lectures all over the world. "This is a place of competition and pressure and responsibility. Students must learn to operate under all circumstances because the outside world is crass, fickle and difficult. One year they love you, and the next year they don't. We try to train them for this, too. To be a professional you need the kind of fibre that can take it. When a student says to me, 'I get nervous at every lesson, Miss Marcus,' I say, 'Fine! Now you know what it is to walk out onto a stage.'"

The brilliant young pianist Van Cliburn, a graduate of Juilliard in 1954, spoke enthusiastically about this balance at the school between study and performance. Shirley Verrett, the highly acclaimed young singer, is a 1961 graduate. She emphasized how grateful she was that Juilliard gave her three months' leave from school to sing with the Cologne Opera, because it gave impetus to her career. "Actually I came to school convinced that I was going to be a recitalist. They pushed me into opera."

Each master teacher restricts himself to a handful of students, because such intimate

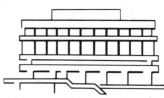

157

teaching is draining. Attention must be complete and interpretation and criticism intense.

"I would like you to have a little more freedom of feeling when you sing," the celebrated mezzo-soprano and teacher Jennie Tourel told a student. "You are a little bit constricted because you really aren't thinking of the words you are saying. Remember, you are presenting yourself to Rodolfo. And when you say, 'la storia mia è breve,' just sing it the way you would speak it: simply, and sincerely." Miss Tourel listened to her student's encore, then added, "Fine, that's much better. However, when you sing, I would like to see an expression of the idea in your eyes. The eyes should be open most of the time to achieve communication with the audience. That is the most important thing in a performer—communication."

So close is this teacher-student relationship that many students consider it inadvisable to be seen talking to another teacher in their field of major interest. Indeed faculty members generally have minimal association with each other. Perhaps that is why there is no faculty lounge equivalent to the student lounge. The thick walls seem to be more important to the faculty than lounges, because they allow each teacher's studio to be utterly private.

Some teachers do reach out for more association with one another. Violist Walter Trampler plays with other teachers in chamber music groups. And it was the violinist Robert Mann who organized the highly regarded Juilliard String Quartet, which plays 150 concerts a year throughout the world.

Trampler and Mann have similar views about Juilliard students. They are not worried about their students' efforts, but they are concerned about their direction. They are afraid that too many students may be searching for the best-paying jobs rather than the best career possibilities.

Near the door of the student lounge are two large bulletin boards offering a wide range of jobs, including babysitting in return for room and board.

One student announced, "Hey, here's a job for a popular clarinetist."

"What's a popular clarinetist?" queried a girl nearby.

"A clarinetist," the boy answered with a grin, "who is popular with people."

President Peter Mennin feels that the discipline and dedication required at Juilliard help counter the success syndrome. For example one of the country's most distinguished instrumental competitions is for the Leventritt Prize. Yet the morning after Juilliard student Pinchas Zukerman won the award, he took up his role again as a violinist in the Juilliard Orchestra.

Deeply concerned about maintaining strict student training, Mr. Mennin reintroduced Solfeggio, a vocal exercise sung by naming the notes. This is a way of gaining fluency in the basic skill of reading music, a skill too many musicians don't possess.

As a composer and teacher of composition himself, Mr. Mennin also brought to Juilliard three of the most eminent names in musical composition: Roger Sessions and Elliott Carter, the great avant garde intellectuals of American composing, and Luciano Berio, the modernist who believes in testing the technical limits of musical instruments.

Though all three men appreciate what Juilliard is doing, they agree that if there had to be a choice they would have preferred to see less money going into construction of the new building and more into grants and scholarships. They point out with some sadness that too many American students still must go to Europe for their initial recognition and development.

This need for exposure and recognition was an early consideration in the development of the Drama Division at Juilliard. The program aimed at selecting the most talented young theater people, and then providing all the necessary help, training and polish to prepare them for jobs in this country.

"Our overall view is to connect the school with Broadway on the one side, and with the entire country on the other," said John Houseman. As Director of the Drama Division, Houseman has an unusually varied background of success in theater, film, radio, television and even opera.

"There's a gap between Broadway and community theaters, and we want to fill it," Houseman continued. "Regional theaters are having trouble staffing themselves, and we want to help staff them."

The basic theory behind the Drama Division's curriculum comes from Michel Saint-Denis. John D. Rockefeller 3rd met him in France in 1958 and brought him here to develop a school program like those he had instituted at the London Theater Studio and the Old Vic Theater. Peter Mennin later appointed him to form an artistic collaboration with Houseman. Saint-Denis's concept called for the kind of training that prepares an actor to do everything—sing, mime, even dance. Out of his previous acting companies have come such artists as Laurence Olivier, Alec Guinness and John Gielgud.

Saint-Denis also believes that style influences life, that the contemporary performer must give his interpretation of the past from the standpoint of the present. "There are not two worlds," he wrote. "There is not a world of the modern and a world of the classic. There is only one theater, and there is only one world."

Houseman accepts only two dozen new students a year in the basic course, another dozen in the advanced classes. Training is intense and imaginative. For example, since juggling demands coordination, releases inhibitions and builds self-confidence, Houseman brought in a circus juggler to teach his students.

In one large studio, students dressed in leotards were stretched out on the floor listening to a teacher detail the proper way to breathe. In another studio, where a group of students were studying improvisation, the teacher was explaining to them how imagination can liberate their bodies, that their use of masks could encourage expressive movement.

"I even hired a well-known burlesque comic to teach them some of his simple routines," Houseman added.

Like the Drama Division, Juilliard's American Opera Center was born brand-new. It's similarly small, with no more than thirty students.

"We do not plan to duplicate existing programs of other music schools or opera companies," declared Tito Capobianco, its first General Director. "We want to be a transition place and a showcase, not simply for singers, but for composers and designers and directors."

Capobianco, of course, is a stage director at the New York City Opera, where he has transformed a number of classic operas with his fresh, distinctive style.

Capobianco explained his approach to opera: "All drama, movement, color in opera comes through the music," he said. "For me every sound in the score must have motivation, every note means something. You approach an opera through the composer and then use the techniques of drama, ballet and painting to recreate his idea. The style of a production always comes to me as I am learning the score. It's like watching a silent movie—the action suddenly begins to run through my head. By the time I am ready to stage the work, I have solutions in my mind for everything —the lighting, the number of steps each character takes, the facial expressions, the movements down to the fingertips. Of course the relative importance of music and drama varies from opera to opera. In a baroque work such as *Julius Caesar*, the vocal line is paramount. First you must have beautiful singing, then music, then drama. With *Tosca*, music parallels drama; for some of the characters acting is more important than singing. Verdi requires great voices even if they weigh 200 pounds, while a lighter work such as *Tales of Hoffmann* needs first-rate acting and singing because Offenbach is a second-rate composer. Mozart is the easiest of all to stage because he designs with a musical line so that everything comes together with absolute perfection."

The American Opera Center hopes to put on four productions a year at Juilliard, not only the masterworks but newly commissioned operas, too, each prepared by a leading conductor and director.

For Opera Center faculty one of the exciting aspects of teaching at Juilliard is that there are two great opera companies across the plaza. Opera Center students hope to sit in on rehearsals to watch and listen and learn. The Center also

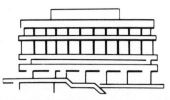

plans to invite some of the great artists from those companies to explain to students just what they will face as working professionals.

Unlike the Drama and Opera Divisions, the Dance Division at Juilliard is not new. It was begun in 1951 with the appointment by Dr. Schuman of Martha Hill as Director. Miss Hill came to Juilliard with a brilliant background as a creative educator in the dance, particularly at Bennington College.

Schuman had written scores for several ballets and was aware of the need for a close relationship between dancers and musicians. The renowned dancer and choreographer José Limón, who also teaches at Juilliard, explained some of the difficulties:

"Musicians sometimes claim that the dancer hasn't the slightest idea of what he wants. But if the dancer is feeling fine in a certain performance and he can sustain higher jumps, he naturally wants a slower tempo. If he's low in energy, on the other hand, he wants the tempo just a tiny bit faster. And how is the poor musician to know all this? Can he read minds? Well, no, but dancers say he can do much better, he can read bodies and their movements."

Anna Sokolow discussed the creative relationship of the choreographer with music. "There must be something in music which attracts me strongly. It must yield images and emotions that I can work with. . . . Sometimes I start entirely without music—but then I begin to hear a certain kind of music, and I go looking for it. Or else, I'll have it composed. Take my Opus 65 for example. I had heard some crazy twist music and I liked it. So I got Teo [Macero] to write some for me. When he saw what I was doing with it, he was the one who suggested adding the Bossa Nova section, which we did. The idea was perfect."

The world-famous Doris Humphrey, who also taught at Juilliard, once said of the perfectly blended work, "that you are not aware where the dance ceases to be and the music begins."

The great difficulty in teaching dance is that so much of it has never been permanently recorded, either by notation or film. This means that the learning must be done mainly "by eye" or "from mouth to foot." It must be imitated and

remembered. And most of the Juilliard students, whether they are studying modern dance or classical ballet, have to "unlearn" much of what they have been taught elsewhere. The eminent choreographer Antony Tudor explained that he prefers to teach "rough clods" than dancers who presumably have a lot more polish. With the polished dancers, he observed, "you have less to get your teeth into."

Before the dance studios at the new Juilliard were ever built, Martha Hill filled filing cabinets with ideas and plans for everything from the placement of mirrors to the construction of floors. Some of the floors were assembled with a layer of concrete topped with wood, then a layer of springs, then resinous powder, then more springs, more powder, and, on top of it all, wood and linoleum. George Balanchine has noted that the floors have a marvelous springy quality.

George Balanchine's School of the American Ballet occupies four of the six dance studios at Juilliard, strictly on a rental basis. The Balanchine School has been generously funded by the Ford Foundation, but Martha Hill's Dance Division has no financial angel and is still a deficit operation.

The Dance Division's financial situation is shaky, but its reputation is secure. The teachers represent some of the greatest names in modern dance and ballet, many of them having their own companies. And graduates of Juilliard have gone into companies all over the world, from Sweden to Israel.

Juilliard's move to Lincoln Center has done a great deal for the school, but it has done even more for Lincoln Center.

"I have always believed," observed Leonard Bernstein, Laureate Conductor of the New York Philharmonic, "that the inclusion of The Juilliard School in the Lincoln Center complex was the ultimate reason for the existence of the Center."

Bernstein's point is that Juilliard represents the potential of Lincoln Center. Juilliard students have played in an orchestra for a special performance of Cosi fan tutte at the Metropolitan Opera Studio. The Juilliard chorus and various soloists have sung in a concert version of Fidelio with the New York Philharmonic. Juilliard drama students watch rehearsals at the Repertory Theater and will probably soon play roles there. Juilliard dance students perform as part of the Lincoln Center, Inc., educational program. And these are only the beginnings of an inevitable blending of talent. Indeed the more Lincoln Center constituents link together, the more important it is for Juilliard to be here.

And as President Peter Mennin put it, "What college ever had a campus better suited to its purpose?"

On the evening of October 26, 1969, ceremonies were held marking the opening of the new home of The Juilliard School and the completion of the construction of Lincoln Center. Shown here are (*left to right*) John W. Mazzola, Managing Director of Lincoln Center; Peter Mennin, President of The Juilliard School; Mr. and Mrs. David Eisenhower; the First Lady, Mrs. Richard Nixon; and John D. Rockefeller 3rd, former Chairman of the Board of Lincoln Center.

BOB SERATING

ALEX SOBOLEWSKI   1

ALEX SOBOLEWSKI   2

(1) Violinist Ivan Galamian, who has been on the Juilliard faculty for 25 years, observes a student during a studio rehearsal.

(2) Mme. Rosina Lhevinne, pianist, has been associated with The Juilliard School for almost 50 years.

(3) Rene Auberjonois coaches students in the Drama Division.

(4) John Houseman, Director of the Drama Division of The Juilliard School.

3

4

ALEX SOBOLEWSKI

MARION TRIESAULT

ALEX SOBOLEWSKI   1

ALEX SOBOLEWSKI   2

(1) An animated conversation between composer Roger Sessions (*right*) and a student. Mr. Sessions has taught at Juilliard since 1965.

(2) At duo-pianos a student is able to work directly with his teacher, here Beveridge Webster (*right*), who has been a Juilliard faculty member for more than 20 years.

(3) Avant-garde composer Luciano Berio teaches composition at Juilliard.

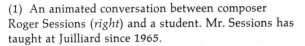

ALEX SOBOLEWSKI

ROBERT ALAN GOLD   **1**

ROBERT ALAN GOLD   **2**

(1) Cellist Leonard Rose listens to a student in his studio, and (2) students of percussion instruments get a workout from Saul Goodman *(back to camera)*, head of the percussion faculty at Juilliard.

(3) Composer Elliott Carter reviews a composition with two of his students at Juilliard.

3

ALEX SOBOLEWSKI

(1) Peter Mennin, President of The Juilliard School.

(2) The Juilliard School.

Some interior views: (3) the Lila Acheson Wallace Library, which houses thousands of recordings, tapes, music scores, and books; (4) a private instruction studio; and (5) a dance studio, with choreographer and ballet director Anthony Tudor, who has been on the Juilliard faculty since 1951, watching over some of his students.

1

2

3

4
5

lincoln
center,
inc.

There were many critics, of course. Most of their comments were what Robert Montgomery refers to as "hat-band criticism."

"It's like saying, 'He's a splendid fellow, but I don't like his hatband.' " Some complained, for example, that the buildings in the Center were too small and others that they were too large.

In his article in the *New Republic* Robert Brustein caustically remarked that Lincoln Center is what the Establishment produces instead of Art.

Of course that is true—the Establishment never has produced Art. All it can do is stimulate the atmosphere and provide the facilities in which Art has the opportunity to grow and flourish. This the Establishment has done at Lincoln Center, and it has every reason for pride.

It has also been said that it would have meant so much more if all the money for bricks and mortar could have been used to commission talented artists to create new operas, new music, new plays, new ballet. But how would that money have been collected? Without the physical fact of a Lincoln Center to stir public imagination, no such sum as $185 million could ever have been raised.

Certainly the tight budget caused compromises on all kinds of things, particularly space and architecture. Certainly there have been strong differences of opinion in the selection of programs and people. Certainly there have been errors of taste and judgment.

But out of this has come a home for our country's two greatest opera companies, our internationally renowned symphony orchestra and ballet company, our finest school of music, a growing new repertory theater and music theater and an innovative library-museum. And out of this has come a handsome, exhilarating cultural complex that has been copied in almost a hundred cities throughout the world.

"I was at a party recently," remembered Tito Capobianco, "and it just so happened that everybody there was a guest of this country—none of us had been born here. And we all decided that Lincoln Center was the center of culture of the new Roman Empire—not only for what it is now, but as a symbol of the projection of American culture. And it's exciting!"

Exciting though the concept is, the sad fact remains that America has no firm tradition of support of the arts. But there have always been dreams.

In 1871 Walt Whitman had his own vision of a cultural center:

"... One stately house shall be the music house, Others for other arts—learning, the sciences, shall all be here, None shall be slighted, none but shall here be honor'd help'd, exampled ..."

And John D. Rockefeller 3rd has thoughtfully said: "So much in human effort today is focused on the material side of life. Assuming people are reasonably housed and fed, what is it for, what is the purpose?"

The philosopher Bernard Berenson wrote just before his death: "All of the arts, poetry, music, ritual, the visible arts, the theater, must singly and together, create the most comprehensive art of all, a humanized society, and its masterpiece, free man."

Yet the miracle is that Lincoln Center was born at all. When the Center was still on the drawing boards, it became apparent that raising money for the fulfillment of the dream would be a difficult task. "You can raise money for Harvard," Clarence Francis observed, "because many people love Harvard. You can raise it for the Children's Hospital, because you can take

people through the wards and show them the children. But who loves Lincoln Center? What have we got to show them? So far it has been only a concept."

But even when the concept reached the construction stage, fund-raising for culture still had to break new ground.

"Lincoln Center is selling a new idea," Edgar Young said. In 1958, Young noted that business support for the Arts was at the stage "where corporate aid to education had been ten years before, and aid to medical and welfare work was thirty years before." More money was initially sought for Lincoln Center from business ($7.5 million) than all U.S. corporations had ever given directly to the Performing Arts in any one year.

According to the *Wall Street Journal* the Lincoln Center idea won its support from the New York business community partly for practical reasons. Project planners estimated that Lincoln Center would attract 2½ million more people every year—an influx that would be a boon to merchants and hotels. Corporations recognized that it would benefit their employees, as well as their customers and stockholders. International companies headquartered in New York noted that Lincoln Center would help the American image abroad.

Aside from the persuasive arguments of self-interest, there was the appeal of a central cultural complex. In a visual world this was a coherent and tangible attraction. Had the constituent buildings been scattered around the city, the most glamorous ingredient would have gone out of the fund-raising drive, and the results would have been doubtful indeed.

The largest corporate gift was $450,000 from Texaco, which already had a long history as the sponsor of the Metropolitan Opera's broadcasts. New York's biggest banks, Chase Manhattan and First National City, gave $250,000 each, setting an example for proportional gifts from fifteen other banks.

But corporate money wasn't enough, and neither were the large sums from individuals. The desperate need was for foundation and government help. The foundations contributed heavily—sixteen of them donated a total of $62.8 million,

the Ford Foundation alone giving $25 million and the Rockefeller Foundation $15 million.

The federal, state and city governments ultimately provided a total of $40.1 million. City money built the Library & Museum and new sidewalks and streets; state money built the New York State Theater; federal funds were funneled in via the Slum Clearance Law, and provided most of the money for the underground garage.

When the fund-raising was in high gear and the construction program became the priority, Rockefeller decided Lincoln Center should have a President with a tough, organized mind and a firm hand. The Board of Directors elected General Maxwell D. Taylor, former Chief of Staff of the Armed Forces. General Taylor arrived on January 4, 1961, but four months later left during the Cuban Crisis, to become military advisor to President Kennedy.

Edgar Young then became the Acting President for an eight-month interim period.

It was during that time that John D. Rockefeller 3rd invited Dr. William Schuman to lunch. Schuman arrived expecting to be asked for his suggestions for a new President, and he had his list ready.

A sharp, analytical man with a warm personality and a lively wit, William Schuman is one of the country's foremost composers. In addition to his nine symphonies he has composed everything from ballet to chamber music to opera. As President of The Juilliard School of Music from 1945, he has helped enlarge its international reputation. And it was Schuman, more than anyone else, who had persuaded the Board of Directors to accept Juilliard as part of Lincoln Center. Now it was Rockefeller who was persuading Schuman to become President of Lincoln Center.

Rockefeller set up the Board meeting, and Schuman presented his ideas for Lincoln Center. Just as Schuman had returned home, the telephone rang. It was Rockefeller and he said, "We want you and we want you now."

Soon after Schuman's appointment the magazine *Musical America* wrote of him, "He brings to Lincoln Center a thorough professional awareness of the artistic opportunities that lie before us, as well as an understanding of the difficult business problems that must be surmounted. . . ." And it added, "a sigh of relief was heard through the musical world."

Schuman took over on January 1, 1962, and the future he saw for the Center was the Rockefeller concept of a whole greater than any of its parts. His vision was that Lincoln Center be more than a collection of buildings—it would be an integrating force for the performing arts all over the world.

It was a strong vision because Schuman is a strong-minded man. And so he made most of it happen.

"I begin with one basic, overriding premise," he said, "that the Arts are crucial to our automated age, that they serve as a creative illumination to counteract the push-button emptiness of our mechanized life, an armor against the disillusionment and anxiety of our times, and an added defense against the destructive forces inherent in man."

Schuman's right hand in the realization of this vision was Edgar B. Young, who for the next four years was Executive Vice President, concentrating on the internal administration and the final construction of Lincoln Center—he was also Chairman of the Building Committee. Young brought in a bright young lawyer named John W. Mazzola. Mazzola is a friendly, forceful man with enormous energy, and the ability to quickly get to the core of a problem. Coming from the law firm of Milbank, Tweed, Hadley and McCloy, Mazzola's initial problems involved taxes, real estate and a mass of corporate legal work. He soon found himself dealing with a dozen different government agencies—city, state and federal. These included the City Planning Commission, the Housing and Redevelopment Board, the Board of Education, the Real Estate Department, the Department of Water, Sanitation, Gas and Electric, the Department of Parks, the Police Department, the Comptroller's Office, the Post Office and even the Elevator Department. Mazzola also negotiated with 24 different labor unions as the buildings opened.

One of the urgent problems was, and still is, street traffic.

"Traffic in the city of New York is a bizarre mess," Mazzola commented, "and yet we at Lincoln Center are supposed to cure all the traffic problems around us immediately."

One of the surprising complications to this problem is affluence. The original traffic planning tied the Lincoln Center area into sixteen bus lines and a number of subway connections, but growing numbers of the audience prefer taxis or their own cars. It is a hard fact that almost half of the city's 12,000 cabs are not in operation after 8:30 P.M. And this fact becomes a bitter one on a cold night when some 10,000 persons may stream out of the various Lincoln Center buildings within minutes of each other.

Mazzola encouraged increased parking facilities, and there are now nineteen garages and lots in the area with space for 4,000 cars. The 800-car underground garage at Lincoln Center is a public facility operated by the city, which means that much of its space is filled by citizens who are not part of the Lincoln Center audience. Mazzola is currently negotiating with the city to transfer this public garage to Lincoln Center, Inc. And to help cut down the need for cabs and cars, Mazzola persuaded the city to provide special buses to transport Lincoln Center audiences to selected stops on the East Side.

In addition to all of these concerns Lincoln Center, Inc., also had the countless headaches of being a landlord. The Board of Directors determines overall policy. John D. Rockefeller 3rd is Honorary Chairman of the Board and Amyas Ames the new Chairman of 33 Directors, 12 of whom represent the constituents, with the Mayor and the Parks Commissioner as ex-officio members. There is also a Lincoln Center Council with a dozen members—the top executive of each organization in the Center, plus three from Lincoln Center, Inc.; they are primarily concerned with areas of cooperation, operational as well as artistic.

Lincoln Center is the landlord because it built the buildings and owns most of them: the Metropolitan Opera House, Philharmonic Hall, The Juilliard School and the Vivian Beaumont Theater. Leases on these buildings run from fifty to a hundred years, on a cost-only, nonprofit

173

basis. Except for Philharmonic Hall all the tenants maintain their own homes. In turn Lincoln Center leases the New York State Theater and sublets it to City Center. The city of New York owns the Library & Museum, and The New York Public Library operates it.

As the landlord Lincoln Center, Inc., supplies general services to its tenants, operating a $4 million central mechanical plant distributing air conditioning (five million tons a season), water, steam and electricity. This costs $325,000 a year to run, and constituents pay for what they use.

Another responsibility of Lincoln Center as landlord is security. Carved out of the heart of a slum area, Lincoln Center found itself with the problems inherent in such an area—from juvenile delinquents to drug addicts. It therefore created its own private security force to patrol the plazas. In addition each of the constituents has security police within its own building. It is thought that the rapid increase in construction and renovation throughout the surrounding area will gradually eliminate the need for extra security. In the meantime, though, Lincoln Center, Inc., feels this is an appropriate function for the city to assume, just as it assumes police protection of other centers of art and learning.

The city does maintain the outdoor plazas: the central plaza; the reflecting pool area in front of the Beaumont Theater; and the newest addition, Damrosch Park. The 2.3-acre park is located in the southwest corner of the Lincoln Center area. It has a band shell named after Daniel and Florence Guggenheim, a lovely backdrop of trees and enough bench space for 4,500 listeners.

Robert Moses had insisted on the park, as well as location. The architects complained because the location limited their flexibility; the Met staff worried about the noise; and the city fretted because the cost estimates kept mounting. The final construction cost was $1,528,769, twice as much as the original estimate, but the Damrosch and Guggenheim families contributed most of the money to build it. Both families have long been associated with New York City music. Frank Damrosch was chorus master of the Metropolitan

Opera from 1885 to 1891 and helped found the Institute of Musical Art, which was later absorbed into Juilliard.

While the city cares for the walking area in Lincoln Center, the Center itself pays for the fountain and the pool. The fountain costs $25,000 a year to operate, and the pool has been a 65,000-gallon problem. It took several years to eliminate a leak, and this postponed the opening of the Footlights Cafeteria underneath.

But all ended well and the Footlights inauguration was coordinated with the completion of Juilliard. The cafeteria seats 250, has a pleasant decor, an area for private parties and even uses white china. Many students come carrying their lunch in paper bags, then buy milk and dessert at the counter. But Footlights is more than a place for eating. Performers and technicians meet there to drink coffee, talk, exchange ideas and enrich their understanding of each other.

Two of Lincoln Center's smaller projects have been highly successful. They are the Gift Shop, begun with a bank loan and now making a modest profit, and the Guided Tours, which break even on earnings of about $250,000. The number of people annually visiting Lincoln Center is now estimated at four million, and it already has become the second most important tourist attraction in New York City (the United Nations is first).

Visitors can be guided by people who speak languages ranging from Spanish to Estonian. Among the diverse group of thirty-five tour guides are an Indian actress, some architectural students, a psychology student studying group dynamics, and Metropolitan Opera chorus members trying to earn extra money. The guides say that visitors are curious about everything from the economical lockers at the Beaumont Theater to the magnificent chandeliers at the Met. A frequent question at the State Theater is "How many beads are in those curtains?"

Answer: Approximately 9,260,000.

Lincoln Center, Inc., has the responsibility for operating and renting two halls: Philharmonic Hall and Juilliard's Alice Tully Hall. Philharmonic

Hall is generally regarded as "overbooked." This means that the hall is booked for more use than it can comfortably handle. But even with nearly 500 performances in an average year, rising costs still leave it a deficit operation.

The resident organization at Alice Tully Hall is the Chamber Music Society of Lincoln Center. This group has become one of the most popular music organizations in New York, and eventually may grow into a separate constituent of Lincoln Center. It now has its own Board of Directors and raises its own funds.

"The thing about our Board," said Edward Wardwell, one of the Chamber Music Society's charter members, "is that money alone can't get anybody on it. Our Board members are not only excited about chamber music, but most of us can play an instrument."

The new Artistic Director of the Chamber Music Society is Charles Wadsworth. A Juilliard graduate (M.S. in piano, 1952), Wadsworth has assembled a resident Chamber Music ensemble of nine performers, with himself at the piano.

"People ask me, 'Well, what are you doing that is so different?'" Wadsworth has said. "I tell them that we are bringing together, for the first time, artists of the highest quality to form a nucleus of musicians who will be regularly joined by distinguished guest artists. In that way we will be able to survey the entire range of chamber music—all periods, styles, combinations—and that this has never been done before."

The Chamber Music Society has commissioned several new works. The first was *New People*, by Michael Colgrass, a lyric composition in a modern idiom set to seven of the composer's poems, and scored for viola, piano and singer. Luciano Berio, who teaches composition at Juilliard, has created a work that features electronic piano and electronic harpsichord. Pierre Boulez, newly appointed conductor of the New York Philharmonic, has also accepted a commission and will conduct the finished work himself.

"The concert hall experience should be joyous," Wadsworth said, "not always dramatic or so damn serious and sad."

While the Chamber Music group was born fully grown, the Film Society of Lincoln Center developed from one of the many projects supervised by Schuyler G. Chapin, then Vice President in charge of programming for Lincoln Center, Inc. Under the guidance of Amos Vogel and Richard Roud, Lincoln Center for five years sponsored an annual film festival. The festival brought a new audience and another art form into Lincoln Center. During that time the Center also sponsored an annual program of exceptional student films and discovered many talented film makers.

The Film Festival was a resounding critical success and, as might be expected, a financial failure. Lincoln Center, Inc., could no longer afford to subsidize it, so if the film program was to continue it had to find its own funds. It was then that Schuyler G. Chapin resigned from Lincoln Center, Inc., to become Executive Director of the Film Society. William F. May, Chairman of the American Can Company, was persuaded to become Board Chairman, with Martin E. Segal as President. (The present Executive Director is Gerald Freund.)

During the early years of Lincoln Center Schuyler Chapin's main concern was the Summer Festival "in which we found ourselves engaged in all sorts of planning, scheming, pulling, tugging, praying, cajoling, pleading and sweating" in order to put it together. It turned out to be the largest international festival ever produced in the United States. In addition to its being big, there was a truly festive air about it all. Colorful flags hung in the plazas and outdoor cafes, and the programs themselves were a veritable cornucopia of the performing arts. There was a choice of great variety: from the daring contemporary repertory of the Hamburg Opera to the familiar strains of *South Pacific*. There was Yehudi Menuhin and the Bath Orchestra; Peter Ustinov's new play, *The Unknown Soldier and His Wife*; films from Czechoslovakia; poetry readings; Ravi Shankar and his sitar; the Promenade music of André Kostelanetz. It combined the old and the new, the popular and the esoteric—all with a spirit of gaiety.

It generated excitement and fun, and *The*

Times headline read:

DEFICIT CAN'T HIDE FESTIVAL'S SUCCESS.

It was a success for the ten thousand people who filled the theaters and the plaza each night.

It was a success for the young people who crowded around the Jazzmobile in the afternoon sun.

It was a success for the thoughtful people who listened to poet Archibald MacLeish open the Festival, saying, "Human understanding is only possible through the Arts. . . .With the Arts, instructed by the Arts, this could become a great, perhaps the greatest Age."

And it was a tremendous success for 800 teachers and administrators from all over the state who had gathered there to listen, talk and learn. The convocation of educators was another effort to expand interest in and understanding of the performing arts. Actors, singers, designers, directors and dancers all made themselves available for general discussions. "It left me breathless," one teacher wrote afterwards.

This kind of communication has reached a unique level in Mark Schubart's educational program for high school students. Schubart's program in the course of a year has taken the performing arts—ballet dancers, actors, singers, musicians—directly to 1.2 million students in a tri-state area.

Mark Schubart is a dynamic man and a former Dean of Juilliard School.

"I never worry about the kid who plays with the school orchestra," he said. "He may or may not get some real feeling for music out of it, but what about the 98 percent of the kids who don't play instruments, and have no idea whether it's something of interest to them at all? And the reason for this is, the Arts are always presented as something you *do*. We teach kids about literature, but never worry whether the kid will write a novel or not. That's not the point. But too many schools feel that this is the point with the performing arts. Now I don't believe the Arts *are* for everybody. Nothing is, including artichokes. But I think that the students themselves should have the right to decide whether the Arts should be part of their lives, and they can

do this when it is part of their school curriculum."

A school of 2,000 students might get six different programs throughout the year for a cost of ninety cents per student. In addition the students are offered reduced-price tickets for performances at Lincoln Center. For many—perhaps most—all this is their first exposure to the excitement of live performances.

Robert Preston, a concert pianist from Juilliard, remarked: "I'd been given dire warnings at times about the restlessness and the boredom, and instead the response has been marvelous. Their discrimination is not an immature rudeness, but rather the result of definite likes and dislikes which they're not afraid to express."

A typical troupe from the Repertory Theater included five performers: Ray Fry, Ann Whiteside, Robert Ackerman, David Sullivan and Rhoda Gemignani. In a rented station wagon with a trunk full of props, they traveled for six months all over the state of New York.

"What it comes down to," said Ray Fry, "is whether or not the teachers themselves are interested in what you're doing. If teachers really are interested, then things are prepared for you, and the kids are aware of what's going to happen, and are anticipating it. You know that for forty or fifty minutes on a stage, you can change these kids' lives somewhat. Then you get comments from kids who say, 'I never liked the theater before, I never wanted to go; but now I'm going.' Kids are so wide-open, you know—their reaction is so honest. One boy wrote afterwards saying Rhoda was better than Bob Hope."

The feeling of the troupe is that this kind of community performing brings theater back to its roots. And faced with a capricious, young audience, artists find it impossible to grow stale.

"School audiences may be the most exacting we ever encounter," said Cynthia Barnett, a young soprano with the Metropolitan. "They are also the most enthusiastic and the most appreciative. Youngsters respond more quickly and more spontaneously to quality performance than adults do."

A student at Northport High School in Suffolk County, fifty miles from New York City, described his reaction to the repertory troupe:

"This guy came out on stage in a turtleneck and we felt very close to him right away, because he looked like one of us. He was real cool."

Then the troupe warmed them up with four different kinds of comedy—from Shakespeare to Shaw to contemporary, and the student audience was with them all the way, reluctant to let them go. There was no scenery, just a few props and some simple changes of costume, but the acting was both broad and personalized, fast-paced and completely captivating.

One of the boys seated in the front row was boisterous and critical before the performance. But he was soon caught up by the comedy along with everybody else, and when it was over, he yelled to Northport's drama teacher, "Mr. McGuire, they were real good! Bring them back soon, willya?"

The idea is not to play down to the audience, Mr. McGuire explained. If a school has a performance of *Cosi fan tutti* scheduled, the music classes play recordings of the opera and hold discussions about Mozart's work. Art classes are introduced to the costumes of that period. History classes learn how opera often pokes fun at the social structure of the day. "It's all very experimental," McGuire added, "but very exciting."

In this simple and powerful idea is the birth of an audience. It also provides the most visible evidence that the strongly individualistic constituents of Lincoln Center *can* work together. The major incentive for cooperation is full funding of the program. Government money pays the performers' salaries and travel expenses, and private funds of the Lincoln Center Corporation absorb the heavy cost of rehearsal, production and administration of the entire educational program.

The Lincoln Center money for such purposes comes from many sources, including a special fund. Speaking before the Economic Club of New York on January 17, 1968, William Schuman observed, "Far from having any hope of making money, our task is to lose money wisely. There is always a gap between what is paid out and what is taken in at the box office." And then he told the story of the wife who could not balance her checkbook. "In response to her husband's

irritation, she turned on him and said: 'Sweetheart, I am not overdrawn. You are underdeposited.'"

A crisis developed, however, when the $12-million special fund for Lincoln Center, Inc., dwindled to almost nothing. For William Schuman the financial crisis meant postponing fulfillment of the dream. The educational program would continue, and grow, because it had a high priority and was so well backed by government and private money; but the administrative staff would have to be cut back, the Summer Festival canceled, the Teacher's Institute postponed, the Film Festival re-evaluated, a dozen other programs placed in limbo.

From a professional standpoint the situation caused Dr. Schuman additional concern. "I have of necessity become less involved with the artistic and cultural phases," he said, "and more and more with the administrative activities, particularly those dealing with the financial problems of the Center." He decided, therefore, that the time had come for him to work again as a creative musician.

It was not difficult to understand his position. Indeed his presidency had stretched into seven years. William Schuman had made his contribution to Lincoln Center—and it was a great one. The Board appreciatively named him President Emeritus.

Moving into the breach as Chairman of the Executive Committee was Amyas Ames. A senior partner of Kidder, Peabody & Co., Ames was President and later Chairman of the Board of the New York Philharmonic. In that interim, too, John W. Mazzola, the former General Counsel, became chief executive officer with the title of Managing Director.

Despite their view that Lincoln Center was "bleeding badly," both men talked with guarded optimism. Ames, who has since replaced Rockefeller as Chairman of the Board of Lincoln Center, has likened the development of the Center to a space project. "It requires an enormous thrust to get the rocket in orbit, and once it's there you have to worry about its direction." The major thrust at Lincoln Center has been accomplished with Juilliard; the physical plant is complete.

The direction, however, has changed somewhat, and the speed has been reset and slowed. The film festival has managed to provide its own financing, but it is still a part of the Center. And Ames has hopes that the cancelled Summer Festival will be revived, though in a different form. Rather than import the great theater and music of the world, he wants to encourage the enormous reservoir of talent within the Center to cooperate in creating their own Summer Festival.

Ames can now think about such programs because the Capital Campaign has been successfully completed, and all the buildings in this $185 million cultural conglomerate are finally paid for.

But there was a critical time when Lincoln Center, Inc., found itself competing for operating funds with its own drive for capital funds.

"The problem was that we had gotten all the government money we were going to get until the buildings were completed," said Mazzola, "and it was the same story with the main money from the corporations. We had to go back to the well and the well was dry. So the first thing we did was tighten our budget, almost strip it. We had to present ourselves as a tight operation, and so we did."

"We then decided to chase the megabuck," added Henry E. Bessire, the former Vice President in charge of fund-raising, who now holds a similar position at Princeton University. "But there are very few people who can walk into somebody's office and ask for a million dollars."

Two of those few are John D. Rockefeller 3rd and Lawrence A. Wien. Wien, the former President of the Federation for Jewish Philanthropies, has said, "I believe you must not only give money for the poor, but you must give money for the future."

"Larry would call some of his real estate friends and say, 'John D. Rockefeller and I would like you to have lunch with us,'" Henry Bessire recalled. "And they would come, and they would listen, and they would give."

Finally $2.5 million was left to be raised. Rockefeller and Wien tried to corral a handful of wealthy friends to pay it off, but even their persuasive powers didn't work. So the two men decided to do it by themselves—each contributed $1.25 million, thus completing the final installment of the Capital Fund campaign.

In thirteen years of fund-raising, the $185 million had come from foundations, corporations, governments and 11,474 individuals. Lincoln Center was finally built and paid for, and without a mortgage.

"Now comes the real challenge," said Mazzola. "We've got the bricks and mortar, but we have to persuade everybody that our mission isn't accomplished—it's just begun! We need operating money. We need money to keep going and keep growing."

Mazzola talked enthusiastically about the eight new members of the Board of Directors—five of them in their thirties, three in their forties. He talked about the new plans for funding the Teacher's Institute, the possibility of chartered buses to bring suburbanites to Lincoln Center performances.

"We're even talking about having an hour show on Saturday mornings, bringing in ethnic groups from all over the city—and especially the young people. Let this be their time with their talent, plus some of their favorite guest stars.

"What we have at Lincoln Center must never be just for the few," Mazzola insisted. "It must be for everybody."

Further recognizing its civic responsibility, Lincoln Center has been an integral part of the Community Council, a citizens' group representing the surrounding sixty-block area. Rabbi Edward E. Klein, the Council's President, stressed that a major emphasis of the group was on maintaining the community's heterogenous quality. The Council also deals with the city constantly on urban renewal, traffic congestion, social welfare, street lighting, tenant evictions, housing for the elderly and the need for a neighborhood center.

"We're an obvious factor in the city's economy," Mazzola continued. "I'm talking in terms of tourists and real estate. Tax evaluations have skyrocketed in this area. New buildings have brought the city more than $20 million in new taxes. By 1972 those taxes will probably be more than $30 million, and Lincoln Center is mostly responsible for that."

Mazzola and Ames hope that much of their budget will be met by patrons, friends and foundations through a campaign of annual gift-giving. They have launched a successful, consolidated, corporate fund drive. This means a single request by Lincoln Center, Inc., on behalf of the constituents, the income of which will be apportioned to all those involved. But both these men also firmly believe that there must be increased government subsidy for the performing arts.

Ames already has made a request for government subsidy to keep our symphony orchestras alive. As Chairman of the Board of the New York Philharmonic, Ames represented the largest symphony orchestra in the country. He dramatically pointed out that construction of a single traffic circle in New York State costs $25 million, a sum which is 2½ times the amount needed to rescue *all* the symphony orchestras in the country for a full year. In Berlin, Munich, Amsterdam and The Hague, Ames noted, symphony orchestras receive government subsidies which take care of 75 percent of their total budget. But in the United States more than 130 symphony orchestras have been financially unable to continue since 1962.

A similar story is applicable to the other performing arts. Canada provides a $30-million subsidy for its arts. If the United States contribution were proportionate to the Canadian, our subsidy would come close to $300 million. Instead the 1969 budget of the National Endowment for the Arts in the United States was only $10 million. Thanks to the fresh effort of Nancy Hanks, new chairman of the National Endowment for the Arts, and Michael Straight, this amount has been raised to $20 million. Representative Ogden Reid noted, however, that the United States still only spent three cents a person for the arts as compared with $5.50 by Austria. "I think the arts have come of age, but they must have a higher basic priority," said Representative John Brademas, chairman of the House Select Subcommittee on Education.

In an excellent study for *The New York Times*, Milton Bracker thoughtfully compared European subsidy of the Arts with ours. He noted that the United States had no nationally supported opera like La Scala in Italy; no subsidized ballet like the Bolshoi in Russia; no state-sponsored orchestra like the Philharmonic in Vienna; and no government-financed theater like the National Theater in London.

Bracker noted with irony that the Chicago Lyric Opera Company did once receive a $16,000 subsidy for the travel expenses of opera singers hired in Italy—but the subsidy came from the Italian Government.

A bleak picture emerges from two detailed economic reports: "Performing Arts—The Economic Dilemma," by William J. Baumol and William G. Bowen, Professors of Economics at Princeton University; and a Rockefeller Brothers fund report entitled, "The Performing Arts: Problems and Prospects."

A study of these reports indicates the following: The income gap in the Arts is due to constantly rising costs, rather than mismanagement or featherbedding; salaries of performers are uncommonly low as compared to other professions; ticket prices, though high, have not risen in proportion to other services and costs; and the actual audience comes from a narrow segment of our population, mainly well-educated professional people in their late youth or early middle age.

That normally small audience segment is further reduced by the high ticket prices, unsafe streets, parking difficulties and traffic. Television and recordings have become an increasingly comfortable alternative. And many of the young are turned off by strictly classical programming; their curiosity is for the new sounds.

The thoughtful people at Lincoln Center, Inc., know all this, and they also know what they must do. They are already doing much of it, and planning more. Mark Schubart's enormously successful educational program has opened up a potential young audience of millions. The Film Society attracts another new sector of the young. The Chamber Music Society, operating at full capacity, attracts still another fresh audience. The proposed program for ethnic groups will bring in an audience from a new direction. And there are many more ideas yet to be tried.

Lincoln Center began as a group of separate, strongly individualistic constituents loosely connected by a common concept. More and more now, however, there has been a growing cooperation and a deepening relationship. Not only do these constituents share air conditioning and security and heat and chilled water, but they find it practical to share a box office at several department stores. Former Director for Productions Robert P. Brannigan, who called himself "the top mop," pointed out other areas of maintenance and supply that might be cheaper if used cooperatively. A central system for mailing, filing and data processing is just one possibility. An organized labor pool is another. It might even be cheaper to get a single contract to wash all the windows.

The constituents work together on the educational program, and they find it works wonderfully well. And if the Met unexpectedly needs a tenor for *Madame Butterfly*, they may borrow one from the neighboring New York City Opera. In return City Opera may borrow some scenery. Members of the New York Philharmonic teach at Juilliard. Technicians find themselves working in several buildings. So may orchestra members and ballet dancers. Young Repertory actors may work as ushers or guides throughout the Center. And the Juilliard students have given

the whole area the tone of a University of the Performing Arts—watching rehearsals, attending extra-curricular lectures, learning the way of the professional.

The artistic individuality of all the constituents is still intact, as it should be. Indeed there would be great resentment if Lincoln Center, Inc., adopted too paternalistic an attitude. Nevertheless the increased sharing and blending of the talent and energies must ultimately result in a single spirit.

Lincoln Center is not simply a cluster of buildings—it is an instrument ready to be used. It has all the talent, all the creative force, all the facilities necessary to become a cultural beacon for the country and for the world. What it must depend on now is awareness and public support. With sufficient funds will come a lesser concern about filling seats, and a greater stress on encouraging new ideas and new directions in all the performing arts.

It was John D. Rockefeller 3rd who summed up the dream for Lincoln Center:

"We are building, not for today or tomorrow, but for a hundred years. We hope Lincoln Center will stand in the eyes of the world as a symbol of our national regard for the Arts, and our recognition of their importance in the lives of the American people."

Lincoln Center affects the community in many ways. Building is stimulated in neighboring areas, and access to the performing arts is broadened through such activities as the Lincoln Center Student Program.

ALEXANDER BURGER
1873 - 1932
A LEADER IN INDUSTRY
AND A DEDICATED CITIZEN OF
THE BRONX WHO BELIEVED
IN AND PRACTICED THE
PRINCIPLE OF EQUALITY IN
EMPLOYMENT, AN IDEAL IN
OUR DEMOCRACY

ALEX SOBOLEWSKI   1

BOB SERATING   2

3

4

(1) On the tenth anniversary of the Student Program, Amyas Ames greets students at Alexander Burger Intermediate School 139.

(2) "I'm a Ballerina in the *Nutcracker Suite*" was painted by second grader Susan Seedman for the Student Art Exihibit.

(3) At Julia Richmond High School, students watch a member of the Juilliard Dance Ensemble make up for a performance.

(4) Juilliard violist Marcus Thompson performs for students at Grady Vocational and Technical High School.

VICTORIA BELLER   1

ALEX SOBOLEWSKI   2

3

(1) A student stage crew working on a Lincoln Center in-school performance.

(2) Mark Schubart, Lincoln Center's Director of Education, surrounded by Metropolitan Opera Studio performers and students at Alexander Burger Intermediate School 139.

(3) Part of the Lincoln Center Student Program is the assigning of Resource Personnel to schools that participate in the Program. The Resource Personnel help students to increase their enjoyment of the performing arts and to recognize their own creative potential. Dorene Richardson, a dance specialist, is shown here conducting a classroom workshop at Morris High School.

1

2

3

(1) Miss Alice Tully with John D. Rockefeller 3rd and John W. Mazzola on the opening night of Alice Tully Hall, September 11, 1969. Miss Tully not only provided the endowment for Alice Tully Hall, but is a member of the Boards of Directors of Lincoln Center and The Julliard School and Chairman of the Board of The Chamber Music Society of Lincoln Center.

(2) The Chamber Music Society of Lincoln Center is the resident organization of Alice Tully Hall. Charles Wadsworth (*standing left*) heads the group, playing both piano and harpsichord. The Society's other artists are (*seated left to right*) Richard Goode, piano; Walter Trampler, viola; Charles Treger, violin; (*standing left to right*) Leslie Parnas, violoncello; Paula Robison, flute; Leonard Arner, oboe; and Gervase de Peyer, clarinet.

(3) The annual New York Film Festival held in Philharmonic Hall attracts thousands of film enthusiasts. Here Jonas Mekas (*left*) film director, critic, and Director of Filmmakers Cinematheque, and poet Allen Ginsberg (*center*) talk with the New York Film Festival Director Richard Roud.

RUDY CHALLENGER

The East River Players theater-in-the-street group, produced by Geraldine Fitzgerald and Mical Whitaker, performing for the community in Lincoln Center Plaza.

INDEX